Living at God's Speed, Healing in God's Time

"*Living at God's Speed, Healing in God's Time* spoke to me as a physician about the importance of trusting in God and finding peace in my own life as I journey through my vocation. The reflections and prayers shared by the authors continue to provide me grace and guidance in my interactions with family, patients, friends and colleagues." Jane D'Isa-Smith, DO, South Pointe Hospital, Cleveland Clinic Health System

"The best part of *Living at God's Speed, Healing in God's Time* is the writing style. It is thoughtful, deep, and yet very understandable. I love the variety of quotes and the places from which the authors draw inspiration. It is a wonderful model; inspiration is everywhere!" Rabbi Stacy Schlein, The Temple-Tifereth Israel, Beachwood, Ohio

"In this thoughtful and inspiring book the authors gently nudge us into an awareness of how near the sacred can be in our daily lives. Poignant examples and invitations to change challenge us to rediscover a pearl of great price in difficult times. This book is a joy to read, offering spiritual strength and a hope-filled vision for the journey." Wayne Simsic, author of *Thomas Merton: An Invitation to the Contemplative Life*

LIVING AT
GOD'S
SPEED

HEALING IN
GOD'S
TIME

Charles W. Sidoti
WITH RABBI AKIVA FEINSTEIN

TWENTY
THIRD 23rd
PUBLICATIONS
www.23rdpublications.com

TWENTY-THIRD PUBLICATIONS
A Division of Bayard
One Montauk Avenue, Suite 200
New London, CT 06320
(860) 437-3012 or (800) 321-0411
www.23rdpublications.com

ISBN 978-1-58595-831-3
Library of Congress Control Number: 2011923256
Printed in the U.S.A.

*To Tina,
JoEllen, and Charles*

Acknowledgments

I owe a world of thanks to many people who either directly, by reading or editing the material, or indirectly through countless conversations, shared in the joy and the agony of writing this book. That said, I sincerely thank the following people: Sue Arnold; Lachelle Bell; Tom Carey; Jane D'lsa-Smith, DO; Joe Eszterhas; Dorothy France; Arnold Feltoon, MD; Denise Geisler; Brian Kessler, DO; Erin Newton, MD; Dot Rogel; Rabbi Stacy Schlein; Wayne Simsic; Paul Susak; John Tobey; Dana Trzaska; Skip Walter; and Brother Anthony Weber, OCSO.

According to Ecclesiastes 1:9, "There is nothing new under the sun." In the spirit of this simple wisdom, I give my sincere thanks to those whose material was used in any way in the writing of this book. I have made every effort to properly identify sources and give appropriate credit. To the unknown authors, contributors, and original sources go my heartfelt gratitude and, where needed, my sincere apology for not being able to locate and credit them appropriately.

I thank Paul Pennick, Dan Connors, and all at Twenty-Third Publications for believing in my work and deciding to publish *Living at God's Speed, Healing in God's Time.* I thank Rabbi Akiva Feinstein for coming along on this journey with me. I am honored and proud to be associated with such a great person and rabbi in the writing of this book.

Finally, I thank my family for their love, encouragement, and patience throughout the writing and publishing process.

CONTENTS

PART ONE
Waiting in hope

PART TWO

Responding with trust

PART THREE

Relationship with God

Foreword

I first met Chuck Sidoti back in 1982, when I was Guest Master and Vocation Director here at the Abbey of the Genesee and he began coming to the Abbey for retreats. We have remained in touch ever since. Chuck is the sort of person who is very much in touch with his feelings and aware of the challenges and contradictions that are part and parcel of a serious spiritual life.

The title of his book, *Living at God's Speed, Healing in God's Time*, is an apt description of his personal journey as a serious and committed Christian.

Living at God's Speed, Healing in God's Time is a series of reflections from his personal life experiences as husband, father, and hospital chaplain, with fellow chaplain Rabbi Akiva Feinstein as contributing author. It is written in something of a conversational style, making for easy reading while at the same time challenging the reader to see his or her own life more from the supernatural perspective than merely the natural. It is a book about achieving freedom from the tyranny of believing one is, or should be at any rate, master of one's destiny. As such it is a book about arriving at a new level of peace.

As Chuck relates it and demonstrates so well in his life, *One of the keys to a more peaceful life is learning when to allow oneself to be led and when to take life by the horns* (Reflection 26). In the monastic tradition, which has been formative in Chuck's spiritual growth, this is known as discernment.

The book, I feel, succeeds admirably in what it set out to do, namely, provide simple ways of letting go of worry in an ever-changing world. I trust you will find it makes for an engaging and challenging read.

Brother Anthony Weber, OCSO
Abbey of the Genesee
Piffard, New York

Above all, trust in the slow work of God. We are, quite naturally, impatient in everything to reach the end without delay. We would like to skip the intermediate stages. We are impatient of being on the way to something unknown, something new, and yet it is the law of all progress that progress is made by passing through some stages of uncertainty—and that may take a very long time. And so I think it is with you. Your ideas mature gradually—let them grow; let them shape themselves. Don't try to force them on, as though you could be today what time and grace will make you tomorrow. Only God can say what this new spirit gradually forming within you will be. Give God the benefit of believing that the Spirit is leading you. Accept the anxiety of feeling yourself in suspense and incomplete.

– FATHER PIERRE TEILHARD DE CHARDIN, SJ

Introduction

▶ CHARLES W. SIDOTI

*Life's constant change is not what matters. What matters is
how we choose to live in the midst of life's constant change.*

Life at God's speed is life in God's time. Over the years I have come
to realize, through my personal life and my experience as a hospital chaplain, that God's time often differs from *our* time. This book
provides spiritual insights that can offer a new perspective about
the constant change that is so much a part of our life's journey,
and that gives many people cause to worry about the future. If you
are someone with a tendency to worry, it is important to realize
that this tendency may never go away entirely, but it can certainly
be reduced to a level where it does not prevent you from enjoying life. In writing this book, I was increasingly aware of a higher
power at work in the universe and within the context and changes
of my own life. That growing awareness has made a profound difference in the way I live. I believe the following reflections can do
the same for you.

Living at God's Speed, Healing in God's Time is arranged into
four distinct parts. Each part represents a key aspect of spiritual

1

growth. The final three reflections of each part are written by contributing author Rabbi Akiva Feinstein, providing a different perspective in regard to the theme of each particular section. Some of these reflections are co-written by Rabbi Feinstein and me.

The primary objective of these reflections is to suggest a way of facing change that can become a new and healing life path. A brief "Connecting Point" section follows each reflection. The purpose is to assist you in thinking about how the message of each reflection might be integrated into your personal life and circumstances. Each reflection ends with a prayer asking for God's help, so that the meaning behind each of the reflections might truly enter into your heart in a meaningful, personal, and lasting way, a way that leads you to continued spiritual growth.

My suggestion is to simply read each of the meditations and see if its message finds a place within you. If you find a connection, an insight that is meaningful to you, just let it remain with you for a while before moving on to the next reflection.

PART ONE

Waiting in hope

No one likes to wait. We often find it difficult to accept, and yet so much of our life's journey seems to involve waiting for God to reveal the hidden meaning behind the changes that take place in our lives. It is important to realize that not all waiting is the same. Waiting on God is not like waiting for a red light to turn green, where nothing really changes except the color of the light. As we wait on the Lord, there are significant and purposeful things occurring behind the scenes. These *things* are God's work taking place within the changes that occur in our lives. The reason you and I have to wait is because God's work is accomplished and revealed to us in the daily unfolding of our lives, slowly and over time. In this section you will find insights that can help you to face the times in which you are forced to wait out a situation, and do so with hope in your heart. It is my prayer that the following reflections will help you see the time you spend waiting on the Lord as a time that is full of promise—God's promise.

1 Trust heals

journeying with faith, hope, and patience

▶ CHARLES W. SIDOTI

Free me, Lord, from the inner bondage and endless cycle of what I think needs to happen before I can be happy. Free me, Lord, from my idea of the solution. Help me to wait with open-ended, joyful expectation; and help me to experience your peace. – CHARLES W. SIDOTI

Ever wish you were more able to go with the flow? Have you ever wished you could go through the day without something upsetting your inner peace? It can be very helpful in this regard to think about how well you process the constant change that life provides. How well you process change has a direct relationship to the level of inner peace you experience.

If you're like most people, you will discover that it is usually easier to talk or philosophize about change than to deal with it when it occurs, especially if the change is unwanted or unexpected. When the ground shifts, and life changes, our clear-sightedness and wisdom, so readily available when all is going well, evaporate, and an inner storm arises. For the moment, we may lose our footing, our sense of being in control.

I have begun to realize, however, that the inner storms we sometimes experience are usually naturally occurring events in the process of human growth. Even the sense of losing control can be an important part of the growth process. This insight is the beginning of a healing process, one that can help us to loosen our grip on the steering wheel of life. An ongoing personal transition can then begin to take place—a transition from fear to trust. I have come to realize that there really is a higher power that remains in control when the things we can do come to an end.

Famous American Catholic writer Thomas Merton, on an audiotape titled *The Mystic Life*, describes the need to feel that you are in control as "a need to see the future before it happens." This is something many of us try to do even though we know that it is impossible. As we gradually learn to trust, our "need to see" starts to become less powerful in our lives. Merton goes on to say, "Realizing that you don't need to see—is seeing, and it can be a very clear form of sight."

This "realizing" can be a very slow process, but just knowing that an inner transformation is taking place is, in itself, healing. It is true to say that the healing each of us desires is being born out of the various struggles of our individual lives, out of the very ground upon which we stand. The more we are able to be attentive to what is happening in our lives in this present moment, the more we will be open and available to receive the gift of inner healing that God desires to bestow upon us.

Becoming a person who is better able to go with the flow is proportional to our level of trust. Trust that the changes that occur in our lives are not just random, chaotic events, as they sometimes seem to be. Trust that there's more to life than meets the eye.

CONNECTING POINT

Believing there is more to life than meets the eye opens the door to the personal realization that life is a sacred journey. It enables you to see beyond the outward appearance of things and to trust in what is yet to come. Trusting that there is more to life than meets the eye is a prerequisite to living a life of hope, making it possible to go with the flow.

PRAYER

Lord, it is obvious that there is much more going on in life than what I am aware of. Help me to believe that more is you. Enable me to trust in your work in my life enough to not need to see today that which you are preparing for my tomorrow. Amen.

2 Living in the in-between time

making things happen vs. letting things happen

▶ CHARLES W. SIDOTI

When we pray the words of the Serenity Prayer, "God, grant me the serenity to accept the things I cannot change, the courage to change the things I can, and the wisdom to know the difference," we present God with three requests.

- The first request is for the ability to accept the things that we cannot change. Here we ask God to help us to entrust those things that are outside of our control to God. And it is right to ask for this, for we need to let God do God's part.

- In the second, we ask God to give us the courage to "change the things we can." In this request we ask God for the courage to do the things that are within our control in order to change those things in our lives that need to be changed. It is right to ask this, for this is our part.

- In the last line, we ask God for the wisdom to know the difference between the two. It is in this final part of the prayer where peace is to be found, because it helps us to separate

7

what is our part from what is God's part. We need to do our part, and we can rest assured that God will do God's part.

It may take what seems a very long time for the work God is doing to evolve to a point where we can perceive it. Often, it is only in hindsight that we can perceive what God has done. It is important to realize that there is an in-between time that we all experience in our faith life. It is the time that comes after I have done what is within my control to change my life, while still waiting on God's part to be realized.

Living patiently with joyful hope in the in-between time can be one of the most challenging and yet most rewarding things we can learn to do. For an action-oriented person, the in-between time can seem like a time in which not much is happening, or at least not happening in the way, or as rapidly, as we want it to occur. If we are experiencing a fearful or lonely period in our life, it can be especially difficult.

This in-between time can seem like an awful desert. We may quickly grow impatient and begin trying to implement changes ourselves. That is certainly not always wrong, but more often than not, actions motivated by our impatience don't obtain positive or lasting results. We need to learn to become more comfortable living in the in-between period, giving God time to do God's part. If we can learn to be patient during this period, we will discover that it is possible to find a balance between when to *make* things happen and when to *let* things happen. We will gradually come to understand that the in-between time that we may perceive as being a kind of down time is actually quite fertile. Things are developing and taking shape during this period, although we may be unaware of them.

The ability to let God do God's part, to be patient during the in-between time, depends largely on whether we really believe anything is happening while we are waiting. There is a classic psychological question you may be familiar with that is related to our ability to wait on God: "If a tree falls in the forest and there is no one there to hear it, does it still make a sound?" To believe that a tree falling in the forest, without anyone there to hear it, truly does make a sound requires a certain level of spiritual development and trust. The answer to this question can be an indication of whether a person truly realizes that he or she is not God, or instead has a false, inflated sense of his or her own importance and ability to control life. It suggests a level of growth in which we are able to perceive God as "Other," and that is significant. It means that we truly believe there is a God who can and does act upon our life in ways that may yet be unknown or at least unclear to us. That belief, that knowledge, makes it possible for us to wait.

Neither making things happen nor letting things happen is right for every situation. There are times when it is appropriate to take action and other times in which waiting a situation out, allowing it to evolve, is the right thing to do. It is important to realize that *both* stances, both attitudes toward facing particular situations, are required of us at different times. It is in learning to discern which manner of approaching life is appropriate for a particular situation that inner peace is to be found. It can be helpful to ask yourself from time to time, in relation to whatever might be happening in your life, "At this time, should I be making things happen or letting things happen? Is what I am focusing my attention on now within my power to change, or is it outside my control?" Trust that the answer will intuitively come to you, and allow yourself to be guided by it.

CONNECTING POINT

Most of the time, giving a situation time to evolve is a good idea. Learn to trust in the slow work of God in your life. Although you may not be aware of it, trust that it is taking place, because it is. How do you want to spend your in-between time: fretting...or confident, trusting that God will do God's part?

PRAYER

Loving God, letting go after I have done what I can, and trusting that you are at work in my life in ways unknown to me, is difficult. Help me to trust during my in-between time so that I may have the peace of mind of knowing in my heart that eventually all shall be well. Help me to realize that your work in my life does not depend on me always being aware of what you are doing. Grant that I may give you the benefit and the respect of trusting that you are doing your part. Amen.

3 Our world, God's world

discovering "who we are"
in God's world

▶ CHARLES W. SIDOTI

Coming to terms with life's constant change is one of the greatest challenges that we face. It is interesting to note, however, that there are many areas of life in which we often have little or no trouble accepting change. Sometimes we welcome it with open arms; at other times we may find it bittersweet. Many parents experience the bittersweet aspect of change as they watch their child board the kindergarten bus on the first day of school. The change of seasons is an example of a change that we often take in stride, accepting it as a natural and even a welcome part of life.

There is another level of change, however, that affects us differently when it occurs, because it *touches* us differently. Changes of this kind are the ones that involve a significant part of our personal world.

We know intellectually that all good things eventually come to an end, but the fact that they come to an end is outside our control. It isn't left to us. Albert Einstein is credited with the statement, "Nothing happens until something moves." There is a lot packed into this short sentence. If it were up to us, certain things in our lives would never change. For example, the people we love would never die.

When significant change occurs in our lives, no one consults us before allowing it to take place. But if we are attentive when "something significant moves" in our world, we will come to realize that the universe is very compassionate, seeming to care very much about *our response.* This is seen in God's silence, patiently waiting for our response, hearing and accepting us just as we are. It can be said that all of life is really about God's waiting and our response, not only to the many changes that continually take place in our personal world but also to the many opportunities for growth that these changes present to us.

Although we sometimes feel left alone to face life's changes, God promises to be with us always. It is through this ongoing process of change happening in our life, followed by our response, that we discover "who we are" in God's world. When we open ourselves to this process, our life becomes integrated more and more into God's larger world. We will eventually discover our proper place in it and find inner healing at a very deep level. We will become aware of our connection with the Creator in a way we never imagined and see life and everything in it in a completely new way.

All of this will come about because God cares enough to allow "something to move" in our world. It is here, in the ongoing process of change, that the faithfulness and mercy of God's promise to lead us touches our lives in a profound and meaningful way.

CONNECTING POINT

All living things change. It is the way of the universe. It is God's way of working in our individual lives as well. Think about the way you feel when change happens in your life. Do you always feel the same, or do different types of change affect you differently? The more you are able to see change, all change, as God working in your life, the more you will be able to see your life as a journey of continuous growth toward what it means to be human and what it means to love.

PRAYER

God of goodness and peace, your love for me and for all of creation is the only thing that does not change. The universe has been changing for countless years. I have been changing since the time I was conceived in my mother's womb. Help me to make peace with the constant change that is part of life. Help me to realize that you are always with me waiting in the midst of the change to give me something new and good. In times of change help me to wait for your love, mercy, and wisdom to be revealed to me. Amen.

4 The acorn and the oak tree

most real learning takes place over time

▶ CHARLES W. SIDOTI

I once heard it said, "Scripture contains the word of God in the way that the acorn contains the oak tree. It is all there, but its presence is made known to us little by little." Living at God's speed means accepting that my understanding of the way God works in my life will come to me *in God's time*. Sometimes the proverbial light bulb goes on in our heads and we learn something instantly, but most of the time real learning takes place slowly, over real time, as our life unfolds. This is especially important to understand in regard to the reading of sacred Scripture.

I had an experience I would like to share with you that might help to illustrate this point. I facilitate the operation of what is called the Relaxation Channel at the hospital where I work as a chaplain. The Relaxation Channel is a closed-circuit television system that is operated within the hospital. The channel is programmed with relaxing and spiritually oriented videotapes offering in-patients an alternative to commercial programming in their rooms.

In setting up the system (prior to DVDs appearing on the market), I had to make arrangements with a vendor to make copies of the original program tapes. The copies would then be run in a bank of VCRs that are used to run the channel so the original tapes would not get worn out from constant use. In all, I was asking the company to copy about one hundred tapes, which I did not think would take very long at all. Having one hundred tapes made would provide enough copies to run the channel for about five years.

I imagined the vendor putting the original and the blank tape into a machine, then a button would be pushed and, *zip*, the tape would be copied in seconds. I figured the turn-around time to have the copies made would be a couple of days at the most. I was wrong. Making each individual copy would take two hours—the actual running time of the original tape. The vendor explained to me that every copy had to be made in *real time*. The recording process was not *zip* as I had imagined.

This experience was a real eye-opener. It is a good illustration of the way God's lessons (often found in Scripture) are revealed to us. God's word becomes part of who we are—in real time—in real life, though we sometimes wish it were otherwise. It is through the interaction with life and the people in our life that we learn the really important lessons. It isn't just a matter of reading it in a book. Even if the book is the Bible, experience with life matters. Here is another story:

> Indeed there is a story about an intellectual youth who felt he could learn everything from books. He read about the stars and became an astronomer, he read about history and became a historian, he read about swimming and drowned. Some things we can only learn by wading in slowly, from the direct experience of the ocean of being lapping against our body. To enter this process

directly is to participate in the healing we took birth for, is to become fully alive.

— STEPHEN LEVINE, *HEALING INTO LIFE AND DEATH*

The meaning of this story is not that you can't sit in solitude with your Bible or some other spiritual book and gain valuable insight. Of course you can. What it means is that some of the things that you read about will only be integrated into your life through your active participation. That is how God chooses to work. Scripture, if it is affecting us in a healthy way, if it is to be a source of lasting inner peace, will direct us to find God revealed within the created world, especially in our relationships with others. Usually this happens slowly, over the course of many years, in the everyday situations of life.

CONNECTING POINT

Grasping a concept or idea intellectually is one thing; having it become a real part of who you are is something quite different. The latter takes active participation in life and is realized in real time—God's time.

PRAYER

God of wisdom, grant that I may give sacred Scripture and other spiritual writing the respect that they deserve. Help me to read with humility, allowing the knowledge you bless me with to move from my head into my heart, that it may truly enter into my life. Amen.

5 The fortune cookie

the great advantage of learning to
wait out a situation

▶ CHARLES W. SIDOTI

*We have what we need. We don't have to rush after it. It
was there all the time. If we give it time it will make itself
known to us.* – THOMAS MERTON

There is wisdom and inspiration all around us, sometimes appearing in places that we do not expect. To my surprise, one of the guiding principles of my life came to me in a fortune cookie!

Now, I'm not someone who normally places much stock in the advice of fortune cookies. I have always considered them to contain lighthearted wisdom or just fun and silly messages. The message in this particular fortune cookie, however, gave me reason to pause. It read, "Do not depart from the path which fate has assigned you."

There are a few ways to look at this statement. On the one hand, it can be easily dismissed, given about as much thought as you would give to reading your fortune on a Bazooka Joe bubble gum wrapper. However, if you look at the statement for what it actually says, instead of where it came from, it can be quite profound and thought-provoking.

The advice of this fortune cookie can be seen as a bold statement that you and I are not just wandering aimlessly through life. Advising us to stay on our current path implies that God is very much aware of who and where we are in our life's journey. The main point is that we need to give life, with all its problems, time to evolve instead of always running after our heart's latest desire or making life-changing decisions based on our fears in the midst of our confusion.

It is true that sometimes a change in direction is called for, and in fact is required of us. However, as a guiding principle, it would be best if we learn not to change direction every time our life path becomes difficult or confusing. Sometimes we need to have the courage to wait out a situation rather than run from it. I have often been pleasantly surprised by the outcome of events that, as they were unfolding, I thought could not possibly lead to anything good. Giving life events time to evolve and unfold is not easy. It is difficult to be patient. This is especially true if we are unhappy with what we see taking place.

We are called to grow in the awareness of God's presence in our lives. There are ways we can help this growth process along. First, we can continue to be faithful to our spiritual and religious practices, making time to pray and asking for an increase in our awareness of God's presence in our daily lives. Second, we can ask God to help us wait out a situation instead of retreating in panic from it. There are many additional ways as well.

The words of a noted retreat master, Father Anthony de Mello, seem appropriate here. They speak of how the awareness of God's presence and God's work in our lives will come to us:

> **Question:** Is there anything I can do to make myself enlightened?
>
> **Answer:** As little as you can do to make the sun rise in the morning.
>
> **Question:** Then of what use are the spiritual exercises you prescribe?
>
> **Answer:** To make sure you are not asleep when the sun begins to rise.

CONNECTING POINT

Giving life events time to evolve and unfold is not easy, especially if we are unhappy with what we see taking place. The benefits, however, of learning to be more patient are tremendous. Have you ever run in panic from a situation and later, upon looking back, realized your panic was not necessary? You can choose to respond differently. You can choose to respond more patiently.

PRAYER

God, whose wisdom fills the universe, grant that I may see in my daily life the thousand ways your wisdom speaks to me in ordinary situations. Help me to be patient. As my life unfolds, may I trust you enough to let it evolve, confident in your guiding presence in whatever happens today. Amen.

6

Learn to appreciate life's natural rhythm and cycles

▶ CHARLES W. SIDOTI

From womb to tomb, our lives are fundamentally affected by the cycles and rhythm of life. The beat of our hearts and our breathing, without which nothing else would matter, are examples of our inseparable connection to life's rhythm. The cycles at work in the world are easy to see. For instance, every day the sun rises in the east and sets in the west, marking the start and end of each new day, a cycle to be repeated far, far into the future. Like the sun's movements, our cycle of rising in the morning and going to sleep each night demonstrates one of many similar cycles present in the workings of the human body. The seasons, the tides, the functions of our bodies—the examples of life's cycles and our connection with them are truly endless.

Reflecting on the cycles that are present in life is worthwhile for anyone who would like to live more peacefully. Becoming more aware of life's rhythm makes it possible for you, in a sense, to enter into the dance of life in a more deliberate way. It will allow you to have a more patient attitude toward life. This in turn can help you to be more patient with yourself and with others. Once you learn to appreciate the natural rhythm and cycles of life, the ebb

20

and flow, then the sense of urgency that can have such a tyranni-cal effect on your mind will begin to slowly diminish. I once heard someone say that there are some things that you can only learn by being alive long enough. Knowing that the rhythm and cycles in your life are precisely the channels through which peace and har-mony will enter your life is one of those lessons.

One of the most profound ways of understanding how cycles can affect our lives is found in the ancient Chinese theory of how things work called *Yin-Yang*. I have found this theory to have invaluable meaning and true wisdom. The symbol that represents this way of understanding is . The outer circle of the symbol represents "everything," while the black and white shapes within the circle represent the interaction of two energies present in our lives, called "yin" (black) and "yang" (white), which cause every-thing to happen. They are not completely black or white, just as things in life are not completely black or white, and they cannot exist without each other. "Yin" represents the movement of energy in our lives that is dark, passive, downward, cold, contracting, and weak. "Yang," on the other hand, represents energy that is bright, active, upward, hot, expanding, and strong.

The shapes of the yin and yang sections of the symbol actually give you a sense of the continuous movement of these two energies, yin to yang and yang to yin. This way of looking at things demon-strates further the understanding of the presence of cycles in our lives. In the yin-yang theory, the cycle demonstrated is between positive and negative energy flowing within our lives. Our moods, our outlook on life, how things seem to go in general, seem to be related to this yin-yang movement from the dark to the light.

Rhythm heals. Why does music make us feel better? It is because rhythm is so basic to the human body and mind. Getting lost in our desires and worries has a way of fragmenting our psyche, causing us to be out of sync, out of balance and out of harmony with the rest of life. We become lost in our minds and imaginations. Music, whether it is beautiful classical music, popular music, or the rhythm of an African or Indian drumbeat, can help to bring us back in sync again. It has a way of de-fragmenting our minds that inwardly heals us.

The purpose of reflecting on, or paying more attention to, the cycles and rhythms so prevalent in life is that you might gradually learn to struggle less against their movement and move more gracefully with them. It is important to realize that life's cycles and rhythms are in large part the way God chooses to work in the world as well as in our personal lives. Remember, God isn't removed from you, sitting up on some throne in heaven somewhere. God, the source of life, is to be found within the created world and life's natural cycles. God comes to you and me from within the very essence of our lives. This is true from the farthest reaches of the universe to your own heartbeat, and your very next breath.

CONNECTING POINT

As you age, becoming more familiar with life's cycles, it is possible to become more relaxed with them, to move more easily with them, resisting less and growing more.

PRAYER

God of spring, summer, fall, and winter, help me to see your presence in the many seasons and cycles of my life. In the lapping of the waves on the shore, in the wonderful rhythm of my favorite song, and in the beat of my own heart, help me to recognize your creative love in the rhythm of my life. Amen.

7
The greatest prayer life...is "in" your life

▶ CHARLES W. SIDOTI

"For where your treasure is, there your heart will be also" (Matthew 6:21). Of all the sayings of Jesus in the New Testament, I think this is one of the most clear and direct. The words of Catholic author Robert J. Wicks echo the same message when he says, "Tell me what you think about most of the time, and I'll tell you who your God is."

In pondering where my own treasure lies, I found myself thinking about my personal prayer time. I asked myself, "Is my personal prayer time the place where my heart's treasure is *supposed* to be?" If it is, then there is a problem. While I definitely find consolation in prayer and consider it a most essential part of my life, I often find it difficult. I find it hard to make time to sit and pray. Perhaps you can relate to this. As soon as I decide that I am going to pray, something else comes to my mind that I just have to do immediately. Some days my time for personal prayer never happens because I do the activity that came to my mind instead. At other times prayer can seem dry and barren, not filled with consolation at all.

I sometimes think, "Is it supposed to be like this? Why does prayer often feel like such a chore?" But I have come to see this

23

struggle in a different way. If our relationship is to be with the "Living God" and not some distant, imagined (pie-in-the-sky) god then it truly must be this way. Think about it: If sitting alone in prayer were always easy, if it were always filled with peace and consolation, it probably would be all we would want to do. Our participation in life and our involvement with other people would decrease dramatically, and we would not seek God there. The difficulty I find in personal prayer, I have come to see as God's way of directing me back into the activity of daily life. God is present there as well as in my personal prayer time.

Don't misunderstand. Our personal prayer time is critically important, and you and I need to persevere in it. We will receive enough consolation from it to keep us coming back. But we also need to realize that the dryness and emptiness we at times experience in our prayer time is normal. It is in reality the best spiritual direction we will ever receive, provided that we interpret it correctly and don't become too discouraged. Remember that God chooses to come to us not only in our personal prayer time, but also in the midst of our daily activity, especially in the relationships we have with other people.

The realization that the dryness I experience in prayer is God's way of directing me to pay attention to what's happening in my daily life has completely changed the way I see my day. The lesson here is to know that whether you are engaged in your personal time for prayer, or in the midst of your daily activities, God is present in that place. As you gradually learn to seek God in daily life as well as during your specifically dedicated "prayer time," you will realize that it is possible to fulfill the scriptural directive to "pray without ceasing" because your life will have become a prayer.

CONNECTING POINT

What is your heart's treasure? Ponder the statement: "Tell me what you think about most of the time, and I'll tell you who your God is."

PRAYER

Lord, open my mind that I may live in such a way that knowing and loving you may truly become the desire of my heart. Thank you for the desire that you have given me to pray to you in moments of solitude. May I also realize and appreciate in a new way that you reveal your presence to me in the activities of my daily life. Open my heart to your presence in my daily activities so that my everyday life may become a prayer. Amen.

8 Multiple truths

accepting the reality of multiple truths
in our lives

▶ CHARLES W. SIDOTI

One of my duties as a hospital chaplain is to plan and conduct memorial services at the hospital when an employee dies. This may happen several times a year. I usually try to arrange for someone to sing a reflective song as part of the service. There are several employees who sing in church choirs, and some who even sing professionally and are willing to share their talent at these special gatherings. I recall when Bernard, who ran the information desk in the main lobby, sang a song called "Life Is Hard but God Is Good." The song was a very moving part of the service. I found myself reflecting on the title of this song after the service was over.

The song title "Life Is Hard but God Is Good" contains two truths, two observations about life, each with something of value to teach us. Life is filled with multiple truths. For example, each of the four seasons of the year has its own unique truth to teach, with winter teaching a truth about death and spring a truth about rebirth and renewal of life. Acknowledging and accepting that there are multiple truths in life and learning to live with this kind of diverse reality have been extremely helpful in my own life. I have also found that this fact, while easy to understand intellectually, is not so easily transferred to the heart, where it really counts and can bring healing.

As human beings, we seem to have a natural tendency to rebel and struggle against the tension created by the presence of multiple truths in our lives. If we can somehow change the way we see them, if we can "let them be," surrendering to their existence and accepting them into our life, we will more readily discover what they have to teach us. We will see much of our personal struggle disappear and find greater peace and harmony in our life.

You can help the insight of multiple truths to take root in your heart and bear fruit in your life. Once our hearts soften and we accept the existence of multiple truths in life, we will need to "make room" for this new awareness within ourselves. According to Thomas Merton, "Realizing or observing something new about life is great, but it is important to realize that we also have a responsibility to 'do the work' that the new insight requires of us—that is our part." When we learn something new about life, we need to "sit with" what we have just learned for a while before moving on or looking for the next insight. Seeing a new stretch of road is fine, but once you see the road you have to walk it.

For example, you might read a book or an article and discover a new insight. It is as if a light bulb goes on in your head. We have all experienced this. For that moment, we see things in a new way. This experience is very gratifying and feels good. But rather than doing the work involved to internalize the insight, we immediately look for another book or article to get another insight and feel good again! Very little growth is actually realized.

Experience has taught me that the way to internalize a new insight is to spend some time with it. Let it evolve within you; just sitting in the light of something you might have recently discovered provides time for it to move from your head to your heart. Dedicating time and reflection to the insight of the prevalence of multiple truths in life is time well spent.

CONNECTING POINT

There is goodness in the world. There is evil in the world. There is kindness and generosity within us. There is also selfish interest within all of us. You and I are not all good or all bad. Just as there is a dark side to the world, there is a dark side to you and me. In both cases, the world and ourselves, we must learn to love and accept the whole package until it is transformed into a new creation.

PRAYER

Lord, there are weeds growing among the wheat. Yet, in your wisdom, you advise that weeds and wheat be permitted to grow together. Help me to love others and myself with that same kind of unconditional love. Help me to live with the contradictions that are often a part of my life, trusting that it is your hand that is guiding the process and that in the end, goodness, love, healing, and peace will prevail. Amen.

9 Life is relational

a deeper understanding of spiritual growth

▶ CHARLES W. SIDOTI

As we learn to live with real humility, we will more consistently find inner peace. It is said of Jesus, "He...did not regard equality with God as something to be exploited" (Philippians 2:6). The life of Jesus has something to teach us about God, and that knowledge is not only communicated in what he said and did but also from what others observed and recorded about him. Observing Jesus' attitude toward life and God can help us to discover who we truly are in relation to God, to other people, and to all of creation. It can help us to learn to live with a true, healthy sense of humility.

If the above Scripture passage does not immediately strike us as meaningful, it is because the human tendency to live our lives as though we are at the center of the universe is so completely entrenched in our nature. It is an unconscious way of living that is simply part of the human condition and exists in varying degrees within all of us. We all have a natural tendency to walk around like little gods, trying to re-create the world in our own image. We demonstrate this behavior when we hold too fast to the way we think things or people *ought* to be. As the noted Jesuit retreat master Father Anthony de Mello once said, "The first step to peace of mind and heart is to resign as general manager of the universe."

Martin Buber, the great Jewish writer and theologian, presents an enlightened philosophy toward life in his classic work, *I and Thou*. This approach to life is the complete opposite of living as though I am the center of the universe. Learning to see life in this way has been a very important part of my own spiritual development. When we are able to approach life from the perspective of an I-Thou relationship, we are more able to see and relate to all that is not "I" with greater respect; we begin to see all of creation as "other" or Thou (God). This is very different from when we approach life as though we are at the center of the universe, where the basic way of relating to life is I-It. Prayer from the I-Thou perspective is transformed from being a wish list into a loving communication with the "Other" (God).

Carl Jung, the famous psychiatrist and psychotherapist, talks about the same human development process that Buber describes as a movement from I-It to I-Thou, but Jung calls it the "process of individuation" (referenced in Edward F. Edinger, *Ego and Archetype*). I think it applies very well here because it is a natural occurrence in human growth and development that is designed to bring us to a new and more mature level of conscious awareness. It is a stage of development in which our psyche shifts from its imagined center of the universe, which serves a useful purpose when we are young, and enables us to take our proper place as a fully integrated human being within the context of a larger world than that of a child.

I have come to realize that this transition requires that we "grow up" in the best sense of the term, or perhaps it is better to say that it requires that we mature as human beings. For some people, this stage of development comes almost effortlessly, and they flow right into a new level of conscious awareness, seeing life and God in a new way. These people are very content and humble in who they are, and typically they are kind and loving to everyone. For many of us, though, to say that it can be a difficult transition is a great understatement.

This transitional stage of human development can be a very challenging and difficult time of growth. In addition to being the topic of much psychiatric research and religious study, the process of individuation also appears as a theme in Greek mythology and sacred Scripture. Let it suffice to mention here that the process of maturing psychologically and spiritually is challenging. If we can somehow resist the urge to panic when we sense this maturing process beginning, we will hopefully begin to realize that it is God who is calling us to let go of our old way of being, to begin to live in a deeper way and with a new awareness. It is like a snake shedding its skin; it doesn't really die but rather transforms. This naturally occurring process of growth can lead us, if we are open, to a "letting go" of our old way of being, and this can be a sweet surrender. God is always in an I-Thou relationship with us. It is within the context of the I-Thou relationship that God says to us in Psalm 46, "Be still and know that I am God."

CONNECTING POINT

As you and I mature, psychologically and spiritually, there is a transitional period through which we must pass. During this time, life may not make sense in the same way that it did before. You must learn to see and relate to the world differently. Your familiar way of seeing things may not work for you anymore. Know that you are not going crazy; you are growing. During this time it is not uncommon for people to experience a measure of anxiety or depression, and this is okay. Know that you are not the first person to experience this. It can be a fearful time, but if you realize that what you are experiencing is actually God calling you into a new phase of your life, you will be able to relax and flow more easily as God guides you through this period of transition. Eventually, the fear will go away and you will discover that you have grown. It is a very positive thing.

PRAYER

Lord, help me not to panic as you guide me into new phases of my life. Help me to know and to accept that I cannot understand everything that is happening to me during the growth process. Instead, help me to trust in the process itself, knowing that it is your hand that is causing the growth occurring within me. It is you showing me who you really are, and who I really am. Amen.

10 I don't understand

...and that's okay!

▶ CHARLES W. SIDOTI

Do you really think you are capable of understanding everything that happens in your life? When the question is posed that way, most people will pause for a moment and then answer, "No." And yet people do worry when they do not understand. Worry is actually a desperate attempt to understand or make sense of a particular situation whose outcome is yet unknown. It always involves a situation that we have little or no control over. Although we don't know what the outcome will be, we often make a prediction in our mind, visualizing a worst-case scenario. I have often read, and have found it to be true in my personal experience, that the majority of the time the predictions we make of impending doom are incorrect.

What do you suppose would happen if you finally admitted to yourself that trying to understand everything that happens in your life was totally ridiculous and you gave up the effort altogether? Would the world still turn without you worrying about it? You might argue that the suggestion to give up "worrying" is one of those things that are "easier said than done." Agreed. The fact of the matter is that you can't give up the habit of worry unless you have something ready to take its place. This is true because worry, as negative as it is, gives you a false or imagined sense of being in control. In other words, we *get something* out of worrying. The only way to give up the habit is to replace it with something better.

In trying to give up your habit of worrying, it is a good idea to start small. Instead of trying to control and manipulate people and events in the direction you think they need to go, tell yourself, "I'm just going to wait and see what happens." If you do this, you very likely will discover that inner peace will gradually take the place of your worry. You will notice yourself changing inside, and the change is spiritual growth. Now that is something better! The more you practice giving up trying to understand everything that happens, the more you will notice an increase (in yourself) in what author Saskia Davis famously calls the "Symptoms of Inner Peace."

A tendency to think and act spontaneously rather than on past fears

The ability to enjoy each moment

A loss of interest in judging others

A loss of interest in conflict

The loss of the ability to worry

Frequent episodes of appreciation

Feelings of connectedness with others, nature, self, God

An increase in smiling

The tendency to let things happen rather than make them happen

The ability to give and receive love more freely and frequently   – SASKIA DAVIS

It is about balance. Trying to understand, trying to make sense of life and its events, is okay. In fact, that effort is required of us, *to a point*. The key to living in peace is recognizing when you have reached that point, letting go, and deciding to trust God with the outcome.

CONNECTING POINT

Today I will not try to understand or make sense out of everything that happens. Instead, I will give situations time to evolve by practicing patience, allowing God time to work. I will postpone satisfying my need to understand, choosing instead to trust.

PRAYER

Merciful Lord, letting go of worry is so difficult. Only with your help can I gradually let go of worry in favor of something better—trust in your work and in your loving care. Put into my heart a desire to grow in awareness of your presence, through which I will finally be able to let go. Amen.

11 Life just happens

the freedom to "simply be"

▶ CHARLES W. SIDOTI

There is really very little that you need to do in order to become more peaceful. One of the most helpful books I have ever read on this subject was written by Gerald May, MD, and it is called *Simply Sane*. On the cover is a close-up photograph of a patch of ground, with a single, fragile blade of a plant that has just burst through the soil from the seed below. The premise of the book, so poignantly captured in the photo, is that the overwhelming majority of life just happens. It is not so much what we do, although our participation plays a critical and important part; and that is the paradox. The fact of the matter is that something outside our human power makes the plant burst forth from the seed. If it does not happen, nothing any human being can do could cause it to occur. It just happens! In the words of Dr. May:

> True growth is a process, which one allows to happen, rather than causes to happen. A seed grows into a plant because it is its nature to do so, not because you or I do it. If a seed finds itself in rich earth, with reasonable quantities of water and sunlight, growth will happen. If we sprinkle the ground with fertilizer, water it regularly

and keep pests away, we become involved in the growth process, and growth may be stronger and richer. We are participating in the growth, but we are still not causing it.

Growth is growth, whether it is plant, animal, or human growth and development. For the most part it just happens. There are things we can and should do to nurture and foster that growth within ourselves. Just as we nurture a plant through fertilizing, watering, and caring for it, we can nurture our personal growth by exposing ourselves to things that encourage that growth. In so doing we participate in the growth process but we are still not causing it. This is an important distinction.

There is a point when our attempts to nurture our personal growth can go a step too far. This may happen when what is behind our self-nurturing, our attempt to change ourselves, is really a deep-seated non-acceptance of who we naturally are. When this happens, we get an image in our minds of what we think we should be. We don't see ourselves as already good, so we set out on a process of self-improvement methods, books, gurus, retreats, and counselors of every sort in order to fix ourselves. Many of us go to great lengths to make ourselves acceptable, at least to ourselves. In the end none of these efforts brings lasting results. We may get a new insight to cling to for a while, but when that wears off we are still stuck with a self we deem to be unsatisfactory. And so on we go to the next retreat, believing it is time to find a new fix.

Making one's life a continuous self-improvement project, something the modern commercial media strongly encourages, is what Dr. May calls "insanity." Living the insanity of non-self-acceptance instead of simply being who we are is very painful. The pain will not be in vain, however, if it eventually leads us to give up the effort.

When and if that happens, we might be able to let go of all the self-preoccupation and learn to simply be.

CONNECTING POINT

The overwhelming majority of life *just happens*. There are things that you and I can and should do to nurture our mental and physical health. But the truth of the matter is that if the sun did not rise in the morning, there is nothing you, I, or anyone else could do about it. What you and I decide to do with each new day we are blessed with is up to us. Our whole life works in much the same way.

PRAYER

God of all of creation, I have no idea how you create life out of nothing. Scientists have their theories, and that is all well and good. But in the end, creation remains a mystery far beyond my ability to understand. Help me to live with a true sense of humility, accepting life as gift and as mystery. Give me a spirit of gratitude that I may grow in relationship with you as my Creator today and every day of my life. Amen.

12 Realize that inner healing is a mystery

▶ CHARLES W. SIDOTI

It is consoling to realize that God will do God's part, in God's time. Real healing, physical or spiritual, is always God's part. In his book *Simply Sane*, Dr. Gerald May makes the observation that while some people are quite willing to take credit for being "healers," others take a more humble approach. The fact of the matter is that when actual healing occurs, something beyond our human powers causes it to take place. If it does not occur, nothing any human being can do would cause it to occur. Healing, like growth, just happens. This is true for physical and psychological as well as spiritual healing. No one ever heals someone else; either healing happens or it does not. In Dr. May's words from *Simply Sane*:

> All that has been said of growing can be said of healing. Too often one thinks of the physician or psychotherapist as "one who heals," *but nobody ever heals anybody else.* Nor does any one person heal himself or herself. Like growth, healing is a natural process, as much an ongoing part of us as the beating of our hearts. If you cut your skin, you bleed for a while, and then the blood clots. *Who or what does that?* A scab forms and if you don't pick

39

at it too much, the cells of your skin multiply, rejoining, covering the broken spot. Who or what does that? It happens. You don't do it; at least not with any will. And most decidedly the doctor does not do it. As with growth, one can only say "Healing is happening." No subject. No object....Sometimes the part of the physician is necessary to the healing process. But without the rest of the healing process, the physician could do nothing but autopsies.

Although most of us have tremendous respect for the role of physicians, it is interesting to observe that the vital role they often provide in the healing process is to bring the injured or diseased part of the body (or psyche) into a state where healing is more likely to occur. Dr. May's explanation of both growth and healing as naturally occurring processes has helped me to better integrate a real spirit of trust in the higher power that exists in the universe. It has nurtured a healthy sense of humility within me.

It helps me to trust that God will do God's part, which is always the larger part, involving those things outside my control. Entrusting the big things to God frees me up to pay attention to, and to participate in, my own growth and healing. In appropriate ways, it allows me to let go of those things that are more appropriate for God to resolve. Understanding that real growth and real healing, for the most part, just happen, increases my sense of gratitude for "who I am," flaws and all. It enables me to see my life as unfolding like a flower or plant called forth by a power greater than myself. Dr. May's insights need not be just food for thought. If we receive his words in the spirit of humility in which they were written, our hearts will be nourished by the simple wisdom they convey.

CONNECTING POINT

There is a type of healing that everyone needs to some degree. It is an inner healing that, when it occurs, enables you to accept and to love yourself just as you are, flaws and all. This healing, just like the physical type of healing that happens to a cut finger, is God's business. It is God's part. Trust that if you do the things that are within your control to help the healing process along, the healing of self-acceptance will happen for you.

PRAYER

Loving God, you come to me as I am. You do not define me by what is wrong with me but instead see me as your child. Help me to see myself as your beloved. Help me to trust in the healing process that is taking place within me. Help me to let you do your work on my behalf. Help me to believe in you the way that you believe in me. Amen.

13 **The watch night**

the anticipation of inner freedom

▶ CHARLES W. SIDOTI

In the hospital where I work as Coordinator of Pastoral Care, I recruit and coordinate a volunteer staff of lay people who receive special training to provide spiritual support to patients and their families. Several of these volunteers are African American. A couple of years ago, in the last week of December, I was chatting with one of the volunteers, whose name is Marguerite. She asked me how I planned to spend New Year's Eve. I responded that I was planning to attend a small gathering of friends and family. I asked her if she had any plans, and she responded that she always went to church on that night.

Marguerite explained that there is a long-standing tradition in the African American community of attending church on the night of New Year's Eve for what is called "Watch Night Service." I remarked that it sounded like a wonderful tradition. I said church seemed like a very appropriate place to welcome in the New Year, give thanks for the past, and join with others in a spirit of prayerful anticipation of the upcoming New Year! Her response to me was, "That is not the only reason we go to church that night."

She told me that the tradition of the Watch Night Service dated back nearly 150 years. It began at the New Year's Jubilee, on New

Year's Eve 1862, when African Americans gathered together, staying up through the night in anticipation of the Emancipation Proclamation taking effect. This proclamation, ending slavery in much of the nation, was made in 1862 but officially went into effect on January 1, 1863, at 12:01 AM. Marguerite went on to share with me that although the tradition of the Watch Night Service was still very much observed in the African American community, few people, even among African Americans and their church leaders, were familiar with how the tradition originally started. I found the story and the meaning behind the tradition of the Watch Night fascinating and filled with spiritual meaning.

I conduct a monthly Continuing Education Meeting that all of the Pastoral Care volunteers are required to attend on the first Tuesday of each month. For the January meeting, I planned to share my recently gained knowledge about the Watch Night Service with the volunteers who were present. As I mentioned earlier, many of them, being African American, had attended Watch Night Services all their lives. When I enthusiastically shared with them how I had recently learned about the Watch Night Service and its connection to the Emancipation Proclamation, they all looked at me as if I was from another planet. As Marguerite was not able to attend the meeting that day (of course), I was left alone to support my claim of a connection between the Watch Night Service and the Emancipation Proclamation. None of the volunteers had ever heard of such a connection. There was some chuckling among them. I felt foolish and quickly retreated from presenting the information and moved on to the next part of the meeting.

The next day, I did some investigating on the Internet. I did a search using the words "watch night service" and "Emancipation Proclamation." Up came several links showing an undeniable connection between the two. Ironically, just as I was reading some of the information, one of the volunteers who had looked at me as if I was crazy at the meeting the day before was walking by my office. I invited her in to review the information that I had found. She was surprised at what she read and asked me to print a copy for her.

The meaning behind the tradition of the Watch Night Service relates to our own thirst for inner freedom today. While the reason African Americans gathered in churches in late 1862 was the anticipation of the abolition of physical slavery, there remain today other types of slavery that can have a tyrannical grip on all of us. The inner slavery of fear, anxiety, addiction, jealousy, lust, hate, anger, blind ambition, prejudice, violence, abuse, and countless other chains holds us in bondage. We are enslaved by whatever negative power grips our hearts, preventing us from becoming the people God calls us to be.

In a very real way, you and I await deliverance from our own inner bondage. Ours is a different Watch Night from the first, in that we are not waiting for a law to take effect to free us from physical chains, but it is the same in our anticipation of a freedom that promises to release us from our spiritual chains. We anticipate the freeing of our hearts and minds by God, who has promised to set us free and heal us.

Hearing the story of how the tradition of the Watch Night Service began has changed the way I experience New Year's Eve. I still appreciate it as a time to celebrate and have fun. However, I now also see it as a spiritually rich time filled with deep personal meaning and hope.

CONNECTING POINT

There are many types of slavery and bondage. Physical slavery is terrible and appalling in every way imaginable, but there are also forms of inner slavery and tyranny. These are the things that keep us in psychological, emotional, and spiritual chains and from becoming the people God calls us to be. But God does call you and me to be free, both inwardly and outwardly. Learn to wait on the Lord in the spirit of the Watch Night, in anticipation of the fulfillment of God's promise to set you free.

PRAYER

God, who set the captives free, instill in my heart a desire for the real inner freedom that only comes from you. Free me from all the things that grip my heart and mind, keeping me from growing into the person you are calling me to become and from experiencing the peace that you desire to give me. Amen.

14 Patience is an underrated virtue

▶ RABBI AKIVA FEINSTEIN
and CHARLES W. SIDOTI

Every day, we face some sort of frustrating delay or obstacle. Too often our response is to get upset at how things are not going our way or are moving too slowly for our liking. These feelings can sneak up and overtake you while you are driving your car, stuck behind a slower driver and waiting for the first possible opportunity to pass. Or they may come in the grocery store checkout line, the one with the unbelievably slow cashier who manages to chat with every customer while snapping her chewing gum...and you are in a hurry. You notice that the line next to yours seems to be moving much faster, so you switch to that one, only to have someone a few places ahead of you request a price check on an item. That brings your new line to a standstill. Looking back at the line you left, you watch as the woman who had been standing behind you completes her checkout and leaves.

The very suggestion that you need to become more patient might cause you to groan inwardly, but the greatest reasons for learning to become a more patient person are your own sanity, inner peace, and well-being. It is true that other people will surely appreciate the change and enjoy your presence more, but the one who stands to gain the most by you practicing patience is you.

When you are facing a situation that requires patience, it helps to realize that impatience never makes things happen faster or better. It only causes agitation, pain, and grief, and serves up failure. Impatience is divisive, separating friends, straining marriages, and breaking hearts. When one is on the receiving end of another's impatience, it is hard not to feel upset and not to think that the whole reason for the other's impatience is that "I am not good enough." When we act impatiently, we become angry and upset, and really need support and love more than anything, but the impatience we express does a fine job of keeping everyone away and making sure that we do not receive that tender listening ear that we really need.

It is only a short step from impatience to rage, and we all know what harm can come from uncontrollable anger. Impatience is like an inner blaze that burns us up without giving off any warmth. It usually takes only a split second for the first glowing embers of impatience to ignite and send flames coursing through us. Before we know it, we're leaning on the horn, or going hoarse yelling at our child or spouse. At this point we don't even recognize ourselves, and there is little to be done but to try to rein in those feelings enough to minimize any damage we might do.

We get into trouble with impatience because of our reactivity. Sure, the issue we face may be real. We're late. We need it *now*. There will be consequences. But whatever the problem, no matter how great or how small, facing it as it exists is hard enough. To make it a lot harder by adding our own impatience is insanity. Reacting with impatience only increases our burden, by adding a whole extra dimension of inner suffering to an already difficult experience. Sometimes it is indeed very wise to choose the lesser of two evils.

We need to make a conscious effort to catch our impatience as it is arising, and to nip it in the bud. We make a first move in this direction by developing our awareness, our sensitivity to the tell-tale signs of impatience at the instant they begin to stir. It will take some effort, but realize that learning to live patiently is a primary key to spiritual growth and inner peace.

The ultimate source of life is patient, and in many ways waits on us. Consider that the earth is estimated to be four billion years old, and the universe even older. Think of the pace of earthly eras, creeping along as slowly as glaciers advancing and retreating. Our minds cannot even begin to comprehend such an expanse of time. God has waited a long time for this short day and this short moment in which you have come to be. You have only recently arrived on the scene but God has anticipated your arrival for all eternity. The truth is, we cannot even apply our reference of time to God's existence, but any way we look at it, God is patient.

And after our arrival, during our relatively short lives, God is patient with us. A particularly strong proof of God's patience is the fact that our lives are sustained even when we do wrong. Imagine a universe where there is absolutely no margin for error, where punishment is instantaneous and total. Thankfully, that isn't the world we live in. God is graciously patient with us, preserving our lives even when our actions hit way off the mark, so we have time to come to deeper realizations, make amends, and return to a straighter way.

The root of impatience is the erroneous belief that we are the masters of our fate. That effectively leaves God out of the equation. When we choose to be patient, our spirit unites with God's patient spirit and therefore with God. When we give in to impatience, we disconnect ourselves from God's patience, and in a real way are on our own. When we choose to wait patiently rather than react with impatience to people and situations we encounter, we act in harmony with the way God's entire universe really works. Our consistently patient response is a visible sign that we are operating from a belief in a higher power at work in our lives, and that there is more to life than meets the eye. By responding with patience to people (including ourselves), and to the situations of life, we include God in the equation—which makes all the difference.

CONNECTING POINT

To act and respond patiently in life is to unite our spirit with the patience of God, which fills the universe. Decide today to do what you can to live more patiently. Ask for God's help with this.

PRAYER

Gracious God, help me to be patient as you are, and in so doing to acknowledge your power and work in my own life and in the world. Help me to wait upon you in my own life and especially in my interactions with others. Grant that instead of my impatience, your love and graciousness might be communicated to others through my actions. Amen.

15 **Perseverance**

the bedrock of Jewish tradition

▶ RABBI AKIVA FEINSTEIN

Abraham Lincoln is widely regarded as the greatest president in American history, yet his career was full of hardship and sorrow. Born into backwoods poverty, he lost his mother at a young age and received only eighteen months of formal education. He reportedly suffered a nervous breakdown at a key point in his life. His political career was spotty until it took off in 1860. Lincoln suffered ridicule for his strangely tall, ungainly appearance. During his presidency, he was vilified by newspapers and politicians across the political spectrum, and had a terrible time finding support anywhere, including from members of his own party and cabinet. Lincoln's famous Gettysburg Address was not considered a great success at the time. Some eyewitness reports say there was little or no applause. Newspaper responses varied from indifference to predictably partisan praise or condemnation. Why did he continue on his political path, eventually becoming the American icon that he is? Lincoln kept going because of an inner conviction that things would get better and that he had a role and purpose to fulfill. He was right.

The electric light bulb, the phonograph, and the radio vacuum tube are only the best known of Thomas Alva Edison's thousands of inventions. But success didn't come easy. Edison was endowed with a capacity to persevere almost as remarkable as his scientific ingenuity. Every one of his discoveries came after thousands of failures. His first phonograph couldn't reproduce the "sh" sound; it couldn't even say "sugar." It took Edison two years of relentless toil before he finally managed to correct the defect. It is understandable why Edison is credited with having said, "Genius is one percent inspiration and ninety-nine percent perspiration." Edison's perseverance was rooted in the hope that the answers he sought were hidden within the created world, waiting to be discovered. He was right.

In 1993, *National Geographic* photographers, some of the best in the business, shot 46,769 rolls of film, about 1,683,600 frames. That year, 1,408 of those pictures were published. If you do the math, you will come up with a rather pathetic percentage of pictures taken to those published. Expressed in baseball terms, it would be a batting average of about .001. "People are always asking me about the f-stop and shutter speed of my pictures," says natural history photographer Frans Lanting. "I tell them: 'The exposure for that photograph was 43 years...and one-thirtieth of a second.'" With odds of getting published like the ones facing the *National Geographic* photographers, why do they bother? They persevere because of a conviction that the right picture is just waiting to be discovered, possibly with the very next shot. Flip through the pages of *National Geographic* and you will see that they are right.

Perseverance is often rewarded. Society tends to resist new ideas, so it is necessary to persevere, putting the new idea before the public over and over again, until the initial resistance is broken down, and it often works. In science, it is often a matter of trial and error, and many experiments are needed before the right method is hit upon. In art and politics, it may be a matter of gaining experience and perfecting one's technique, things that don't happen overnight. In all of these examples, the rewards of perseverance, whether in the realm of politics, science, or photojournalism, are about the physical world that we can see, touch, and measure. What about perseverance in regard to spirituality or spiritual growth?

The gateway to holiness

It is a misconception that some people are just more spiritual by nature than others, that spirituality is meant for some but not for others, that spirituality is something you either have or you don't. The truth is otherwise. Perseverance is an important key to spiritual growth. Indeed, it is the gateway to holiness.

The Patriarchs we read about in Scripture, Abraham, Isaac, and Jacob, would never have succeeded in founding monotheism and the Jewish people had it not been for their extraordinary perseverance. Tradition records that Abraham withstood ten major trials: two periods of exile; the two abductions of his wife Sarah; the binding of his son Isaac; the sending away of his son Ishmael; the war with the four kings; the prophetic vision of his descendants' enslavement and exile; Nimrod's attempt to murder him; and the danger of undergoing circumcision at an advanced age.

Likewise, Abraham's son Isaac suffered persecutions at the hands of the Philistines, underwent the trial of being bound as a human sacrifice (called off only at the last moment), and was separated from his beloved son Jacob for thirty-six years while his other son, Esau, tried to kill him. Jacob, too, endured a life of physical and emotional hardship. He was persecuted by his brother and swindled by his father-in-law; his only daughter, Dinah, was raped; and for twenty-two years he mourned for his favorite son, Joseph, thinking he was dead (he had been sold into slavery in Egypt).

These were trials that would have broken the spirit of most people. But the founders of Judaism eventually achieved their world-changing goal of establishing the Jewish people and spreading the great monotheistic idea. In times like theirs, for people to persevere through such hardship as they did without becoming bitter, depressed, and sour on life—a reason to hope was needed. At some point it became necessary for them to let go of their need to understand why bad things happened and allow themselves to be led through their tribulations in a spirit of trust. In so doing, they were strengthened and made whole by the struggle itself, for God was present in the very midst of it. In the end, it is always surrender to a power greater than ourselves that holds the real key to perseverance and provides real reason for hope.

"Faith" is a mistranslation

The word "faith" is an English word. In Hebrew the most similar word is *emunah*, which like the word "faith" means "trust in God," but it arrives at this idea in a different way. The root of the word *emunah* is *umanut*, which means craft. That is because in Jewish thought, belief in God is like a craft, a skill, or a set of techniques that are studied and perfected over time. It's not something that you're either born with or not, like a beautiful voice or a great fastball. *Emunah* is a life process; it is a process in which our active participation is required. The end product of that process, that craft, is development of one's own more spiritual self—spiritual growth.

The skills of faith are developed and strengthened in the practice of everyday Judaism. For example, in *Shema Yisrael*, the central affirmation of faith, we twice daily declare the Torah's own formula for coming close to God: "And you shall love the Lord your God with all your heart, and with all your soul, and with all your might."

How are we to reach such a lofty level of attachment to the Almighty? How is a finite being, immersed in the aspirations and woes of the human condition, to reach so close to the Infinite? The answer lies in the next line: "And these words shall be on your heart."

The classic rabbinical commentators write that words of faith should be subjects of continuing meditation, throughout the day, as if they were written on one's heart for constant reference and review. Rabbi Yitzchak Hutner noted that it says, "And these words shall be on your heart," rather than "in your heart," for a definite reason. These lofty ideas often do not penetrate right away but in the course of time. If you continue to say them, ponder them, and keep them on your heart, the right moment will come, and they will make their way into your heart. It is in our rubbing against the events of our daily lives while keeping the words of faith close to our hearts that real spiritual insight, the transformation of our minds and hearts, happens. We see the world with new eyes from an enlightened perspective.

You don't have to be a certified patriarch to get somewhere in the realm of spirituality. The prayers and deeds of ordinary people are fully potent; all that's required is sincere and persistent effort. The great Hasidic rabbi known as the Kotzker Rebbe was once approached by one of his followers, who complained that despite his best efforts, he was unable to summon the appropriate feeling to go with his prayers. They came out empty and lacking enthusiasm. The rebbe told him not to worry, as these prayers were never wasted.

The secret of perseverance

The history of the Jewish people itself is a record of awesome perseverance, a record of a nation never giving up on its divine mission despite two thousand years of exile and persecution.

Perseverance is a built-in feature in Jewish tradition. The prayers for both private and communal needs, for health and knowledge, for the rebuilding of Jerusalem and the gathering in of the exiles, have been offered on a daily basis for more than two millennia.

Perseverance is rooted in hope, and hope is rooted in the belief that things will get better. This is essentially a religious belief, since there is no reason, logically speaking, why things should not continue to get worse. The daily newspaper headlines support having such a pessimistic outlook. The secret of perseverance, however, is that it demonstrates an underlying hope, an inner belief that there truly is a God who is good, and therefore, things will ultimately turn out for the best. Belief in the hidden yet very real presence of God in our life is why perseverance in our struggles, whatever they may be, is completely logical.

CONNECTING POINT

Practicing the virtue of patience, as discussed in the previous reflection, is a sure way to unite our spirit with the patient spirit of God. It is also what makes perseverance possible. Patient hope that God will open a way through what seems impossible to pass through will never be disappointed. Even if the way leads through death, it will end in new life.

PRAYER

God of hope, give me the ability to let go of my need to understand why bad things sometimes happen; and instead help me to allow myself to be led through my time of difficulty, trusting in your guidance and love for me. In the midst of my struggle, help me to hear your voice calling me into your way of peace. Amen.

16 **Like a shepherd**

▶ RABBI AKIVA FEINSTEIN
and CHARLES W. SIDOTI

The Psalms are unique among the books of the Bible, revealing a mysterious healing quality in their ability to connect with us at a personal and profound level. It is not uncommon when reading the Psalms to find that the words give expression to our most human emotions at the very core of our being—emotions that range from the deepest, darkest despair to the most exultant, liberating joy. The ability of the Psalms to connect with us, in many ways, also heals us. As we prayerfully read them, we find that it is the spirit of God with whom they connect our mind and heart.

Psalm 23 is one of the most popular psalms, as well as one of the most comforting. It opens with the familiar words, "The Lord is my shepherd," and many people have found that they do not need to pray the entire psalm to experience its healing power. Simply saying the words, "The Lord is my shepherd," is often sufficient to turn our attention toward God; and turning our conscious attention toward God is a simple, pure, and powerful form of prayer.

The Twenty-Third Psalm can provide immediate help in difficult moments. When we find ourselves facing a stressful situation, speaking the words, "The Lord is my shepherd," can help us to let go long enough to see how God can act in our lives. It can help us to let go of the sense of urgency that we often feel toward a situation, giving God room to work without our anxiety-driven interference. When we say, "The Lord is my shepherd," it is really the same as saying, "I trust you, God," while at the same time expressing a willingness to wait on the Lord. In many of life's situations, after we have done what is within our control, waiting on the Lord is precisely what we need to do.

Psalm 23 is sometimes associated with death. There is a great scene in the 1997 film *Titanic* in which Jack (Leonardo DiCaprio) is anxiously pushing his way through a long line of terrified passengers, all of whom are rushing to reach the highest end of the doomed and rapidly sinking ship. Someone in the death march just ahead of Jack is heard reciting the Twenty-Third Psalm. The person is shown reading the psalm while slowly marching, saying, "Yea, though I walk through the valley of the shadow of death...," to which Jack shouts out, "Hey, would you mind walking a little faster through that there valley!"

In the Jewish tradition, Psalm 23 is commonly included among the prayers that are said during the period of time surrounding a person's death. It is recited in the House of Mourning during the time of *Shivah*. The Hebrew word *Shivah* means "seven" and refers to the seven-day period of formalized mourning by the immediate family of the deceased. Likewise, the Twenty-Third Psalm is often recited at Christian funerals. For many mourners, it can be very comforting, allowing them to be assured that their loved one is being taken care of by God, even though the person has passed from this life to the next.

Yet the words of this particular psalm do not speak primarily about death. They are clearly spoken in reference to life and living. They speak about how God directs, anoints, and comforts us, and of God showering us with kindness.

There is only one clear reference to death. It is the earlier mentioned, familiar verse, "though I walk through the valley of the shadow of death, I will fear no evil," and even this reference is veiled. The Hebrew word *tzalmavet*, though commonly translated into English as a reference to death, would more accurately be translated here as a "dark and shadowy place."

The Twenty-Third Psalm certainly is comforting in regard to facing the final death that we all will experience one day. It is important to remember, however, that its application to daily living, its comforting words telling of God's promise to guide and shepherd us through the many shadowy and dark periods that we all experience, make it a powerful prayer that can provide hope and reassurance today. There are countless small "deaths" that we experience during the constant change that is so much a part of life. The promise of the Twenty-Third Psalm is very much for the living, in this world as well as the next.

CONNECTING POINT

The Psalms possess a special healing quality in their ability to connect with our emotions. Discover that power for yourself by prayerfully reading them on a regular basis. The Twenty-Third Psalm is especially comforting. In its words we find God's promise to guide, protect, and lead us as a shepherd guides his or her flock through life's many changes; and it challenges the dark, shadowy periods and the "deaths" in life.

PRAYER

Merciful Lord, so often I resist your lead, impatiently trusting instead in my own understanding and my own schemes to make things happen. And so you wait on me to trust in you. Help me to let you be the shepherd of my life. Help me to hear and respond to your voice and to accept your guidance. Help me learn to wait patiently on you in hope, trusting that the good things that you promise will be given, and to let it be in your time. Amen.

PART TWO

Responding with trust

The reflections in this section focus on the way we choose to respond to life. Have you ever thought of having a trusting attitude as a choice that you make? It is. It is true that much of what happens in life is outside of our control, but not everything. Every situation contains an element that is within our power to change if we desire to do so. That element is the way in which we respond to the situation. The way we approach life and approach God, at a deep level, involves a choice.

For this reason, giving some conscious thought to "how" you want to "be" in this world is critically important to your spiritual growth. For example, you and I can choose to be open, striving to respond with an attitude of openness to the lessons that life has to teach, or we can choose to close ourselves off, taking a defensive posture toward life. It is not always easy, but if we desire to remain open to life's lessons, we can learn to do that. It is within our control whether we try a new approach to a situation or problem, or choose instead to remain rigidly set in our familiar way of responding. The point is that you have a choice in how you respond to life. That choice will ultimately make a difference in the progress of your spiritual growth and therefore the level of inner peace you experience. My hope is that the reflections that follow offer some helpful insights that will, in some way, inspire and encourage you to choose to remain open on your unique path through life.

17 **Prefer trust**

how trust helps us to live
in the present moment

▶ CHARLES W. SIDOTI

Wouldn't it be nice to look forward to the future with hope, expecting good things? The following reflection is about the way we choose to stand before an uncertain future.

One morning when I sat down to pray, I noticed that it was much easier for me to worry than it was to pray. It seemed that I actually preferred my worry over my usual five minutes of quiet centering prayer. In the midst of this, a wise saying that I have always admired came to my mind: "People have a hard time letting go of their suffering. Out of a fear of the unknown, they prefer their suffering that is familiar" (Thich Nhat Hanh, Buddhist monk and poet).

I find it is especially gratifying and affirming when I can apply such an insight, one that I have sometimes shared with others, to my own life. At these times, I have to take my own medicine. That's okay, because it is important for me to know that the things I write and talk about are not only in my head but are also rooted in my heart. When the above quote came to mind, I was able to understand for the first time why I was finding it easier to worry than to let go and open my heart in prayer. It was because the act of worrying actually did something for me. It gave me the illusion that I had more control than I really did.

Although this illusion is at the same time a kind of suffering, it is one I am familiar with. You do get used to, and in a strange way comfortable with, your own suffering. The mental connection that occurred between my worry and the quote helped me to realize how I was susceptible to preferring my "familiar" worry to the vulnerability involved in letting go of it for "the unknown." This enabled me to let go and assume a more open posture for the remainder of my prayer time.

In reference to the same observation of the disdain we often tend to have for the "unknown elements of life," world-renowned psychoanalyst Erich Fromm once wrote:

> We become necrophilous, lovers of what is dead (the past, the settled, the inanimate, the secure, the already determined), rather than biophilous, lovers of what is living (the future, the unsettled, other people, living beings, the new, the uncertain). Instead of enhancing the possibilities for growth, we limit the situations of life to the familiar, to what seems already well under control.
>
> – FROM *THE HEART OF MAN*

The good news is that becoming aware of our own defensive posture can be the first step toward changing it to a more open, less defensive, more trusting outlook toward the most important day of our lives—*today!*

CONNECTING POINT

We choose the way we face the future. Trust is always a choice. Trusting that God is at work in your life and that good things will eventually come is something that is within your control. Deciding to trust is your responsibility.

PRAYER

Loving God, without you I can do nothing. Help me to realize that you have already given me all that I need to live a life of trust. Awaken in me the desire to trust you. Then, Lord, help me to trust you enough to face the future with confidence and hope, expecting to find your presence and peace, both along my journey and at the journey's end. Amen.

18 Decide not to be preoccupied

focusing your attention
in the present moment

▶ CHARLES W. SIDOTI

Sometimes one of the most difficult things to do is to be mentally present where you are physically present. For example, you may be at home with your family, but your mind is still at work. You are with your friend, spouse, or children, but your mind is someplace else. Maybe you are thinking about some problem that you think you must solve or an encounter you had with someone during the day that is still troubling you. Whatever it might be, it has your attention, and where you are here and now does not. Once in a while this happens to everyone, but to live like this day in and day out is a big roadblock to experiencing inner peace and having meaningful relationships. If your spouse, friend, or child is telling you something important and you are nodding your head but really not hearing or absorbing anything they say, don't you think they can tell?

It is important to understand that there is no real communication happening in this type of scenario. There is no real relationship happening, either. When you are lost in your imagination, reliving

65

some part of your day, mentally trying to solve some problem, or worrying about something that might or might not happen in the future, where are you—really? We do not encounter God when we are lost in our imagination, endlessly reliving the past or worrying about the future.

If you believe in God, ask yourself this question, "Where is God to be found?" God is found and encountered when we are in a relationship with life, and this can only happen when we are present in the moment. Being in relationships with other people requires us to be mentally engaged where we are physically. Don't the people in your life deserve that much? Realize that in addition to others finding their relationship with you much more satisfying, you personally will reap great benefits by choosing to live more consistently in the here and now. You will benefit by experiencing the greater sense of peace that having more satisfying relationships brings.

So how do we make a change for the better? As with anything you would like to change about yourself, the first rule is to be gentle. It is important to realize that a certain amount of preoccupation is natural, even important. It is part of being human. You are supposed to think about things, life events, encounters with other people and problems at work. It is natural for you to process these thoughts in your mind. As with everything, it is a matter of balance. It only becomes a problem when we acquire the habit of constant preoccupation. When we are always or frequently preoccupied, our relationships suffer. Our sense of well-being also suffers, because we are out of balance.

Begin by simply noticing when you are with another person and find yourself thinking about something else. When you become aware of it, gently bring your attention back to the person you are with and what that person is saying. When you do this, you have made a decision not to be preoccupied at that moment.

This does not mean that you will not return later to the thought that was distracting you. You may very well need to do so, at a more appropriate time. It simply means you have chosen to give your attention to what is happening here and now. You will not need to look for opportunities to do this. Once you make the conscious choice for the here and now over preoccupation, after a few times you will naturally begin to notice when you are preoccupied and would rather not be. Choosing to live in this more balanced way, you will be aware of God's presence in a more frequent and powerful way.

There are also times that we might consciously choose not to be preoccupied when we are alone. Constant thought and preoccupation can keep you from seeing and appreciating the presence of God in the world around you. It can keep you from becoming aware of God's presence, because even during your time alone you can still be lost in your own thoughts and imagination in a habitual way. It doesn't only happen when we are with others. When we allow ourselves to be habitually preoccupied, we have left God's world behind and have chosen to live in our own world instead.

The more we make the decision to pay attention to what is happening in God's world, and delay our personal preoccupation until a more appropriate time, the more likely the choice to live in God's world will become habitual. Think of it, habitually choosing to pay attention to the here and now, the place where God dwells. Sounds like a pretty good idea.

CONNECTING POINT

Living at God's speed means deciding to make a conscious effort to give my attention to the here and now most of the time. It means that, for me, thinking about what is happening in this present moment takes precedence over my tendency to think about the past or worry about future events.

PRAYER

Loving God, my relationships with family members and friends require me to be present to them if those relationships are to grow and have meaning. Enable me to give the people in my life the attention that they deserve. Help me to realize that you are to be found within my relationships—relationships that can only take place in the here and now. Amen.

19 Just do the opposite!

step out of your world to a new perspective

▶ CHARLES W. SIDOTI

Over the past several years, *Seinfeld* has become one of my favorite comedy shows. If you're not familiar with *Seinfeld*, it is a rather zany sitcom about the daily life of five single people living in New York City. Perhaps it is more accurate to say it is about their *trying* to have a life.

In one of my favorite episodes, two of the main characters, George and Jerry, are talking at a table in the café where they hang out. George complains, "My whole life is wrong." He elaborates for about two minutes about how everything he thinks and does is totally wrong.

Jerry, listening to all this, suggests to George that if every natural impulse he has is wrong, all he has to do is "do the opposite," which will obviously be the right thing, and his life should be great!

This instantly connects with George, who enthusiastically decides to follow Jerry's advice. George becomes convinced that doing the opposite of everything he thinks will fix what he considers to be his miserable life. Still sitting at the booth and encouraged by his new and fantastic insight, George eyes a beautiful woman sitting at the counter who has just turned and smiled at him.

George says, "Did you see that? Ordinarily, I would feel totally inadequate, not say anything to her, and hate myself for the rest of the day. But not today! I'm going to do the opposite!" He gets up, marches over to her, and speaking with complete confidence, introduces himself as "George, a short, unemployed bald man who still lives at home with his parents." And then he asks her for a date!

Shockingly, she responds favorably! As the show continues, George does the opposite of his natural inclination in several situations, with stunningly positive results. Admittedly, this may be a ridiculous oversimplification of reality, but might this crazy story contain a useful insight for living? I think it does. It points out the benefits of sometimes deliberately responding to a situation in a way that is the complete opposite of how we normally would.

In the story of Martha and Mary (Luke 10:38–42), Jesus comes to visit the home of the two sisters. While Jesus is there, Mary sits at his feet listening to his words. Martha, on the other hand, is busy serving their special guest and doing the many practical things that need to be done when a visitor comes to a home. Martha complains to Jesus that he should ask Mary to help her with the work. Jesus responds to Martha's complaint with a gentle rebuke, "Martha, Martha, you are worried and distracted by many things. There is need of only one thing. Mary has chosen the better part, which will not be taken away from her."

The image of Mary sitting at Jesus' feet is often used to represent the contemplative life, a life focused on prayer and beholding the presence of God. The image of Martha is often used to represent the active life, a life grounded in service to others and doing the many practical things that need to be done. It is not Jesus' response that I want to discuss. I want to focus on the fact that both Martha and Mary were simply doing what came naturally to them. Sometimes in order to live in peace with others, and also as a means to spiritual growth, it can be beneficial to do the opposite of what comes naturally.

I can relate to Mary. Being somewhat of a contemplative, I enjoy doing things like writing and going to a Trappist monastery for personal retreat time a couple of times a year. I'm not too keen on doing domestic chores like working in the yard and do-it-yourself home projects, things that my wife, Tina, loves to do. Here, for me, a little doing the opposite of what comes naturally is certainly a good idea, and I am working on it! Trying something different, something that you would not normally do, can help you to see life from a new perspective.

Wanting to put this idea into practice, I recently signed up to be an usher at my church, something that I ordinarily would not think of doing. Normally, I volunteer to do things like giving spiritual presentations or writing an article for the church's quarterly news-letter, things more in line with my natural inclinations.

I made arrangements to train with one of the experienced ushers. Next, I followed one of the ushers actually doing the job during Sunday Mass. I noticed that while ushering, I did not have the luxury of sitting in the pew with my family focusing my atten-tion on the Mass, as I enjoy doing on a typical Sunday. Instead, I was busy doing many other things, making it possible for those who were sitting in the pews to have a beautiful and spiritual experience.

I thoroughly enjoyed ushering. It was spiritual, but in a way that was new for me. I found it interesting and good to participate in the Mass in this new and different way, seeing things from a different perspective. I will not be ushering every Sunday, mind you. I'm on the schedule a couple of times a month, and when I'm not on duty, I will be sitting in the pew participating in the Mass in my usual way. I have come to realize that the things that come more naturally to me, like public speaking, doing presentations, and writing, are still an important part of me that I can give to others. However, doing something different like ushering helps me to realize that I am but a part of a larger whole and helps me to better see my relationship and responsibility to the community.

In *Seinfeld*, I'm not sure that George had such a noble reason for deciding that he was going to start doing the opposite of his natural inclinations. But can you at least see how the premise of this comical story, "just do the opposite," might provide a useful insight to a new awareness? This simple realization is a central theme found in major religions, is psychologically sound, and is a key to knowing inner peace.

Can you think of an event or activity that you normally don't get involved with that you might consider trying? Perhaps charity fundraisers like walking for cancer or diabetes? If involvement in these types of activities already comes naturally for you, maybe volunteering to lead a committee at work or your place of worship or accepting a public speaking engagement might be the opposite for you. Whatever it might mean for you personally, the point is that whenever you put yourself in a situation where you are able to see life from a different perspective, it can help you to see beyond the limits of your personal world and grow in the essential realization that you are not God. By responding differently from how you normally would, you are not only thinking outside the box, you are stepping onto a new path. And that can make all the difference.

CONNECTING POINT

In addition to the many outward things we can respond to by "just doing the opposite," we can also look inward at our own feelings and reactions to apply this principle. For example, the opposite of responding with fear, anger, and resentment is responding with love, understanding, and mercy. The opposite of impatience is patience. Recall Albert Einstein's definition of insanity: "Doing the same thing over and over again and expecting different results."

PRAYER

Lord, give me the courage to live in the freedom of being a child by sometimes responding spontaneously to the events and people in my life. Help me to experience the newness of life that comes from seeing things from a different and fresh perspective, which doing the opposite can provide. Amen.

20 A fist full of peanuts

the great advantage
of learning to "let go"

▶ CHARLES W. SIDOTI

Living a life where trust is the guiding principle will ultimately require that we *choose* to trust. I have noticed, however, that at those times when I have asked God to increase my ability to be trusting, the request is usually answered with increased opportunities for me to practice trust. That really wasn't what I had in mind. I was assuming that God would answer by zapping me with more trust, after which I would suddenly live in a more trusting way, worrying less and relaxing more. I am now convinced that it isn't going to happen that way.

Learning to trust in God involves acceptance. It means accepting things, people, and life in general, without always feeling that I need to change everything to the way I think it should be. On the other hand, trusting God more will always involve my participation. Living with an attitude of trust is not a passive thing, where we sit back as spectators and think, "God will take care of everything," so we need do nothing. It involves living out the wisdom and balance of the Serenity Prayer, "God, grant me the serenity to accept the things I cannot change, the courage to change the things I can, and the wisdom to know the difference."

Acceptance almost always involves letting go of something. It may be letting go of a fear or worry, or an obsessive desire for a life situation to be different. Or it may be a need for someone to respond to us differently. I once heard a very helpful story about letting go. The story posed this question, "How do you catch a monkey in India?" It explained that the way people catch monkeys in India is to glue a baby food jar onto a stump or large rock, put a few peanuts in it, and leave the lid off. When the monkey comes along, wanting the peanuts, he slides his hand into the small opening of the jar. Grabbing the peanuts, he closes his fist around them. Once the monkey makes a fist to grasp the peanuts, his hand will no longer fit through the opening of the jar, so he cannot pull it out. He is caught, and very upset.

What is so ironic in this story is how easy it would be for the monkey to free himself and go back to enjoying his life. All he needs to do is simply let go of the peanuts. But he will not.

When I notice myself preoccupied with a desire or need to have something be a particular way, I reflect back on this story. I visualize myself like the monkey, with my fist in the jar, holding on to what I desire. This imagery has helped me to let go of my particular desire and to enjoy life again. It sets me free.

CONNECTING POINT

What is your "fist full of peanuts"? What are you holding on to today—that has you caught? Try to imagine yourself letting go of your peanuts (your situation or desire) and moving on with your day in peace.

PRAYER

Lord, often I am so convinced about what I think I need. I have my fist wrapped tightly around a particular desire. Help me to loosen my grip and to eventually let go so that I might enjoy the inner freedom that comes with knowing myself to be a child of God. Help me to desire that which will really bring me peace, and to trust that you will fulfill that desire in your time. Amen.

21 Mind over matter

...the way things are

▶ CHARLES W. SIDOTI

My father had a saying that he would sometimes jokingly remind me of when I would express my displeasure about something. He would say to me, "You know, Chuck, it's mind over matter. If you don't mind, it doesn't matter!" Over the years I have come to realize that there is real wisdom in that little phrase.

Have you ever noticed that for some people, "everything matters"? Behind this attitude seems to be a deep-seated desire to re-create the world according to the way they feel it should be. Practically nothing in life ever really measures up to their standards. They receive very little cooperation from the rest of the world in carrying out their many reconstruction projects. This is a very difficult way to live.

There is another very simple, common saying that contains a pearl of wisdom: "It is what it is." I first heard a friend say this to herself when faced with a situation she wished could be different. As she said the words, there was a noticeable peacefulness, an attitude of acceptance, that came over her that I had not seen during the entire time I watched her struggle against the situation. It occurred to me that this phrase, if spoken sincerely, has the power to heal us. "It is what it is" can imply a realization, an acceptance of the way things are. It can suggest one's willingness to make the best of the situation and move on, rather than brooding about it or trying to change something that cannot be changed.

But living more peacefully obviously involves more than just remembering phrases and clichés or even verses of Scripture. It means living with an openness of heart in which we allow ourselves to be guided by the wisdom of the words that we believe to contain that wisdom. The ability to let go and put these words into action is related to what we really believe about life. I may claim to believe in God, but do I act in a way that bears witness to that belief? A good question to ask oneself is, "Do I really believe there is a plan for my life other than my own plan?" The answer to this question is a key component to experiencing inner peace. If I really believe there is another plan, another power at work in my life, then I probably will not be as upset when *my* plan does not work out. I will not mind so much if I believe that God's plan takes over where my plan leaves off or even fails.

I once heard someone say, "When you change the way you look at things, the things you look at change." Believing that there is a higher plan, God's plan, at work in your life changes the way you look at the future, and your future changes. When I am living at God's speed, the things that matter to me change; they lessen in number because I have become more discerning in regard to what really matters to me. I choose to give my attention to those things because they are truly important.

CONNECTING POINT

It is helpful to realize that you cannot change *every* situation that is not to your liking. Nor should you try. Trust in the slow work of God in your life. God's work in your life is real, even though it is not apparent to you. It is something that you can rely upon.

PRAYER

Lord, as I go through this day, help me to realize that there is another plan at work in my life—your plan. Help me to know when to say, "It is what it is," and to let go of my compulsive effort to change things. Help me to trust that you are working from within the situation that is troubling me. Strengthen my heart that I may trust in your guiding presence in my life today and place my future in your hands. Amen.

22 Resisting the "jack-in-the-box syndrome"

we are called to grow

▶ CHARLES W. SIDOTI

Believing that it is possible to change, that it is possible to become less fearful and controlling and to become more trusting and free, is an important first step toward a meaningful life transformation. It was my wife, Tina, who helped me to see this truth in a new and interesting way. Tina once said to me, "You should not respond to the events that happen in life like a jack-in-the-box." I immediately received a mental picture from this simile and saw it as a wonderful way to see the responsibility we have to grow as human beings. I pictured in my mind the jack-in-the-box children's toy, the familiar colored box with the crank on the side that plays music as you crank it until the top flies open and "Jack" springs out and surprises you. The point is when you turn the crank, you get the same response from the toy every time! As human beings we can, and indeed must, grow and learn to respond differently to the things in life that *turn our cranks*. We are not jack-in-the-boxes.

A day or so after my wife used the jack-in-the-box example, the chief executive officer of the hospital announced her intention to resign and go to work at another hospital. I had known the outgoing CEO for many years and knew that she valued my position as hospital chaplain. I was not at all sure the new CEO would value my role in the same way. I was worried that I might lose my job.

As soon as I heard the news, I went into the hospital chapel to mentally process the information. I felt the familiar sense of panic begin as I thought about all the possible implications for my job with a new CEO taking over. Then, the jack-in-the-box story popped into my mind. I literally found myself asking God to help me not to respond like a jack-in-the-box. Conversing with God in prayer truly helped me open up and realize that there were many other possibilities that lay beyond my own negative thoughts about the situation. It freed me from the endless cycle of reflections about what "I thought" needed to happen in this situation. With the help of the jack-in-the-box imagery, I decided not to panic, but instead to wait. I was able to allow the event to take its course as I looked for God's hand and God's plan within the unfolding events. This event affirmed for me that there really is a plan greater than mine at work in my life, a plan I can rely on and trust in. It is God's plan.

CONNECTING POINT

Think for a moment about your own responses to the events and people in your life that turn your crank. Do you often respond in the same way to them? Choose to live in the dignity that is yours by realizing that you have a choice in the way you respond. Exercising your right to choose your responses instead of just going with your same familiar knee-jerk reactions can be the key that unlocks the door to a whole new passageway, a whole new way of approaching life's circumstances.

PRAYER

Loving God, thank you for calling me to grow as a human being. I do not always live out the dignity that you have blessed me with by calling me to be your child. Help me to live in the freedom for which you created me by responding to the events and people in my life thoughtfully, and not like a jack-in-the-box. Help me, Lord, to believe and to trust you enough to wait and allow your plan to evolve from within each situation of my life. Amen.

23 Row toward the shore

the call to actively participate in life

▶ CHARLES W. SIDOTI

Trust demands action. That action may consist of waiting with hope for events to unfold, or it may mean having the courage to do what is within my control, or as the Serenity Prayer says, "to change the things I can." But trust, indeed, demands action.

I recall reading on a plaque a brief maxim that makes a tremendously important point about how to live an authentic spiritual life. Pictured on the plaque is a man in a small rowboat. He has a concerned look on his face and is rowing hard because a storm has developed on the lake. The caption below the picture reads, "Pray to God…but row toward the shore." I don't know who wrote it, but it is said to be a Russian proverb. Its wisdom very poignantly describes the mystery of what it is to be human and how God chooses to be involved in our lives. The words echo the great wisdom of the Serenity Prayer in affirming that we must entrust to God those things we cannot change. At the same time, however, we have a responsibility to do the things that are within our control, to change the things we can. In this way, we become participants, not merely spectators, in God's world as we grow day by day in relationship with the Living God.

Entrusting the things we cannot change to God and waiting with an attitude of hope are difficult concepts for most of us to put into practice. There is an audiotape on this topic made by the late Fr. Henri Nouwen called *A Spirituality of Waiting*. In it, he explores what it means to "actively wait with hope." In one section of the lecture, Nouwen describes the difference between hoping and wishing, stating that hope is related to trust, trust that God will eventually bring goodness out of whatever we are experiencing, even though we don't know exactly how it will come about. Nouwen defines "hope" as being open-ended, and he relates hope to trust; he relates "wishing" to fear. Unlike when we hope, when we wish we want very specific things to happen, and if they don't happen we fall into despair. Thus, there is an important difference between hoping and wishing.

Having a trusting attitude requires doing whatever is within our control to change the things we can. This is not easy by any means, and it often requires courage. Whatever might currently be challenging us, there are things we can do. There are things within our control that we have a responsibility to act upon. The response of other people to what we do is outside our control. Gradually a rhythm will develop in our lives as we discover we can entrust those things that are outside our control to God, while having the courage to do those things that are within our control. Learning to live in this way has deepened my relationship with God and my trust in God. Remember, whatever issues, struggles, or storms might be happening in your life, by all means, "Pray to God...but row toward the shore."

CONNECTING POINT

God has God's part to do in your life. God's part includes those things that are outside your ability to control or to change. You have your part, the everyday things you have to do such as caring for yourself, your family or going to work. It is also your part to do the best you can to live in peace with others. If you trust God to do God's part, you will discover the virtue of hope growing within your heart. Making a commitment to doing the ordinary things in your life to the best of your ability while leaving the rest to God is to work with God in a meaningful way.

PRAYER

Lord, I have done a lot of wishing in my life. Wishing seems to come much easier than hoping. Help me to trust you enough to become a person of hope, a hope that is rooted in a belief in your love for me. Give me the courage to do my part in life, the everyday things and duties that are my responsibility, and to find a simple joy in doing them. Lord, help me to discover the rhythm that comes with really working with you in my life. Amen.

24 Who is your God?

growing beyond images of God

▶ CHARLES W. SIDOTI

Our religious and spiritual practices are meant to help and heal us. One of my duties as Coordinator of Pastoral Care is to give educational presentations for hospital staff, patients, and the general public. In one of these presentations, I ask the audience members to consider two questions in relation to their own spiritual paths or religious beliefs. The first is a two-part question: "Does your own religious tradition, spirituality, or philosophy of life bring you inner peace? If not, what good is it?" This is often a very sobering question. Along with asking the question, I usually comment, "However you might describe your belief system is well and good! But if it brings you no peace, why do you bother with it?" If we read spiritual books, what motivates us to read? Do we need to find support from a spiritual writer who tends to see things the same way we do? Is your religious practice helping you to grow, transforming you as a person for the better, or do you attend church, synagogue, or mosque because it is expected, and simply fulfills a culturally imposed obligation?

My question came from a scene in the movie, *Brother Sun, Sister Moon*, a 1972 Franco Zeffirelli film about the life and spiritual conversion of St. Francis of Assisi, a reformer in the Catholic Church and founder of the Franciscans. Immediately following his conversion experience, St. Francis, speaking to a group of people gathered outside a church, asks, "If your religion brings you no peace...what good is it?" This question has life-changing potential. It can help us to be open to the wonderful gift that religion is intended to be in our lives. Rephrased, the question might be: "What do you really want or what are you hoping to gain from your religion? Is it to grow, becoming more fully human and fully alive? Do you hope to become a more loving, accepting, and gentle person? Or are you looking for something else?" At a deeper level, isn't this question really asking you and me, "Who is your God?"

The statement of Robert J. Wicks mentioned earlier, in Reflection Seven, brings clarity to what St. Francis is trying to get us to see. "Tell me what you think about most of the time, and I'll tell you who your God is."

The second question I ask people to consider is, "How do your spiritual practices or beliefs affect the way other people feel when they are around you?" This, too, is a very grounding question. Do my religious practices help me to become a more loving, kind, and accepting person? Does my religion help me to have a generative attitude toward others, one that affirms and nurtures other people's growth as human beings? Or does my religion provide me with a reason to feel better than others?

The goal of religion or any healthy spirituality is to help us to rediscover our connectedness to everything around us, but especially to God and one other. It is to help us realize that there are invisible ties binding us together. In fact, the more enlightened we are, the more humble we will become. We will consider ourselves better than no one. We will notice a growing sense of gratitude and appreciation for the gracious free gift of life.

CONNECTING POINT

Today, give some thought to what motivates your interest in religion or spirituality. You may find good, honest, simple intentions are what motivate you. Great! You may discover that your intentions are not as pure as you thought, and that is great, too! Bringing such intentions out into the light will provide you with the opportunity to ask God to help you to make some adjustments if needed, and that will help you to grow.

PRAYER

Living God, free me from any illusions and false images I may have about you. Help me to know you as you really are. Put into my heart a desire to seek you in my life in all simplicity, truth, and, above all, love. Amen.

25 You gotta serve somebody

choosing the direction of your life

▶ CHARLES W. SIDOTI

"If it does not please you to serve the Lord, decide today whom you will serve" (Joshua 24:15). This is an illusion-shattering statement. It is a statement that requires a response because it is born from a fact of life. Since it is obvious that I did not create myself, it follows that there must be a power greater than me at work in my life. Whether I realize it or not, my place as a human being in the midst of creation is a very humble one. The statement requires us to make a choice about what our lives will *mostly* be about. Will my life be about learning how to love and living in harmony with others? Or will it be about getting what I want while looking out for Number One?

As part of my studies to become a chaplain, I came across a fascinating term that is similar in meaning to the quotation from Joshua above, in that it brings us to the same question. The term is "fundamental option." It means that each person has a fundamental choice to make about the overall direction of his or her life. Will you spend your life learning to love others and yourself, or will your life be about getting what you want?

There is a comforting aspect to the teaching of "fundamental option." It is that once a choice is made regarding one's "fundamental option," it is difficult to change. Take, for example, a spaceship that blasts off from Earth, gaining speed and momentum as it travels. Once the spaceship's motion is set, it may get dinged or bumped a little off track, but because of its growing momentum, its overall direction is not easily changed. In this same way, if I decide that my "fundamental option" in life is to become the person God calls me to be and I commit my life to that purpose, then even though I may be dinged and bumped along the way, I can trust that the overall direction of my life will lead to God.

Bob Dylan seems to speak about this same basic, fundamental choice in life in his song titled "Gotta Serve Somebody." The overriding point that Dylan makes in this song is that no matter who you are in this life—rich, poor, powerful, or just an average Joe—your life will, in the end, be lived in the service of someone. Dylan proposes that our lives will serve either the one with the power of darkness in this world or the one with the power of goodness. Like Joshua, he drives home the point that the content of our lives will, when all is said and done, serve somebody.

Joshua tells us, "If it does not please you to serve the Lord, decide today whom you will serve." How blessed we will be, living with renewed confidence, when we are able to speak from our hearts with the prophet Joshua, "As for me and my house, we will serve the Lord," and proclaim this statement as our "fundamental option" in life.

CONNECTING POINT

There is just no getting around it. Your place in the universe, like mine, is that of a created being. There is an additional element that comes with being human that is not found in the rest of creation, that of truly having a free will. This means that you do have a "fundamental option," a choice to make about the overall direction of your life. Today, think about who you want to serve with your life. Because, truth be told, you did not create yourself, so you are "gonna have to serve somebody."

PRAYER

Creator of the universe, Creator of my life, the very desire to know and to love you comes from you. Give me that desire. Help me to want to serve you, to choose you as you have chosen me. Help me to know who I am, Lord, in relationship to you, and let that be enough for me. Let me say with my heart and profess with my life, "As for me and my house, we will serve the Lord." Amen.

26 A personal Egypt

God's guidance in our journey toward freedom

▶ CHARLES W. SIDOTI

One of the keys to a more peaceful life is learning when to allow oneself to be led and when to take life by the horns. Both of these inner actions are necessary at different times. When we reach a point within ourselves where we are able to live in the middle, between the tensions of when to relinquish control and when to assume it, we will have found the place where real spiritual growth becomes possible. We discover a kind of rhythm or dance of life in which we sometimes follow and sometimes seem to lead. In both actions, we are active participants in life.

In my daily work coordinating a hospital pastoral care department, my job is to provide for the spiritual needs of all faith groups. The program serves patients, families, and members of the hospital staff. The hospital does not have a religious affiliation, and that has been a true source of personal blessing to me. In order to serve the many different faith groups represented in the hospital, I have had to learn about them. One of the most powerful insights I have learned involves the Jewish celebration of the Festival of Passover, also referred to in the Jewish tradition as "the Festival of Our Freedom."

Through my association with Jewish friends and colleagues and in researching the significance of Passover, I have found great spiritual meaning in seeing Passover as a distinct action and gift of God in human history prior to the establishment of Christianity. Researching Passover has enabled me to see it from a different perspective, thus gaining a new appreciation for it.

The Jewish Festival of Passover is a joyful time. It is a time for retelling and remembering the story of the Exodus of the Jewish people from both the physical and spiritual slavery of the Egyptians several thousand years ago. The story is symbolically retold in the ritual Seder meal that is observed by whole families during the festival, which lasts several days.

The great Jewish phrase that captures the spiritual meaning is, "We were slaves to the Pharaohs in Egypt, but the Lord led us out of there with a mighty hand and an outstretched arm" (see Deuteronomy 26:8). In my research, I discovered that the message of Passover, "God leads God's people," is not only about what happened in Egypt in the now distant past. The message for us is that "Egypt" is in our own hearts. Each one of us has his or her own personal Egypt. The things that enslave us are the things that keep us from fully developing and living in the freedom and harmony that God calls us to live. They are the negative powers that grip our hearts and create our own personal Egypt. The same God who led the Jewish people out of Egypt with a mighty hand and an outstretched arm wants to lead us out of the Egypt of our own closed hearts so that we may live in the freedom of the children of God. With God's help, we can open up and allow ourselves to be led.

As a Christian, I have found it helpful and interesting to observe that the Last Supper actually occurred on the first day of Passover. I feel a special connectedness with my Jewish brothers and sisters as I wonder if at the Last Supper, Jesus was observing the Passover meal, sharing the Seder meal with his friends for the final time.

Opening my heart to the Jewish celebration of the Festival of Passover has been powerful and insightful. It has been and remains a tremendous source of comfort and healing in my own spiritual journey.

CONNECTING POINT

The same God that led the Jewish people out of the slavery of Egypt many years ago, holding out "a mighty hand and an outstretched arm," reaches out to you today. It is your responsibility to reach back (in prayer) to God in response. God wants to lead you into freedom from whatever grips your heart (fear, anxiety, anger, resentment), preventing you from being the person God created you to be.

PRAYER

Loving God, as you have always revealed your presence to your people, reveal yourself to me. Help me to reach out to hold the hand you offer to me. Lead me to the freedom of mind and heart that you desire to give me, and help me to accept it into my life. Amen.

27

Being open to the spiritual wealth others have to offer

▶ CHARLES W. SIDOTI

Our first task in approaching another people, another culture, another religion, is to take off our shoes, for the place we are approaching is holy. Else we find ourselves treading on another's dream. More serious still, we may forget that God was present before our arrival. – RAYMOND HAMMER

Far and away one of the most helpful things we can learn on the path to inner peace is to appreciate the religious beliefs of other people. I have been blessed in many ways as a hospital chaplain, and one of the most powerful ways has been the exposure to religious traditions and beliefs that are different from my own. My personal faith and religious formation is that of a Catholic Christian, but as a hospital chaplain I am called upon to serve people from various faiths. My role is to help them to get in touch with their own spiritual resources, which may involve different religious practices and beliefs, and to help provide for those specific needs. Sometimes I am invited to participate in those religious practices. These times have been a priceless opportunity to learn about other faiths and to grow spiritually by transcending the religious barriers that tend to keep people apart.

I have always been interested in learning about other religions, and I would like to tell you about one special person who was a catalyst in my learning process. Early in my career, I began developing a volunteer hospital ministry program and was looking for candidates to participate in it. The requirements to become a volunteer in the program were simple enough. The requirements included: the belief in a loving God, the understanding that involvement in the hospital ministry had nothing to do with proselytizing or imposing one's religious views on others, and the willingness to learn about other faith traditions by going through the required training program. The first person to apply was Sue Arnold, the hospital's medical librarian. Sue is Jewish, an active member at temple and also a Holocaust educator. She is a wonderful source of knowledge and freely shares what she knows with others; she is a true educator.

Her involvement in the early development of the hospital ministry program helped to raise my awareness of the need to be sensitive to the traditions and beliefs of Jewish patients, families, and staff (and also of other non-Christians). Sue's presence helped to assure that any ideas, presentations, or teaching that would take place in the program would focus on the spiritual and not so much on the religious aspect of pastoral care. This is something that I would have tried to do anyway, but being able to filter my ideas for the program through Sue's eyes helped to ensure that things would not be presented in a language and format that had even a subtle Christian bias. This is critical to the success of a hospital ministry that is called upon to serve people from many different religious backgrounds. In addition to helping orient the program in the right direction, Sue introduced me to the Jewish faith, something I am forever thankful for because it has greatly enriched my life.

As coordinator of pastoral care at the hospital, I am sometimes called upon to conduct memorial services and other types of religious services for the hospital staff, patients, and visitors. Unless a service is specifically for a particular faith, such as a Communion service for Catholics, my goal is to have it be an interfaith experience, where people from any religious tradition will feel welcome and included. Sometimes I work with members from the local community clergy in developing particular services. Most of them are very happy to participate in developing an interfaith service and it turns out beautifully.

There was one time, however, when the interfaith spirit was not present. A local church leader who wanted to conduct a community prayer service in honor of the annual National Day of Prayer contacted me. She had already been in touch with several church leaders and was calling to invite me to the planning meeting. At the meeting, I noticed that there were only Christian clergy represented. I listened to the ideas being presented about planning the service. It sounded like it was going to be a Christian service pure and simple. No one brought up that since this was to be a community event, it was only right to include clergy from the community's other religious groups in the planning.

I mentioned that I had noticed there were only Christian clergy represented at the meeting, and that as a hospital representative on the committee, I needed to be sure the program would be a true interfaith event in order for me to participate.

The immediate response I received seemed cordial enough. One person spoke up, saying, "Yes, we probably should do that to be politically correct." Someone else chimed in, saying, "Okay, we will invite the rabbi and the imam to be correct, but we [Christians] are all grounded in the truth. We all know what it's really all about." I felt like I was at an "Old Boys' Club" gathering where it was assumed that everyone felt the same way.

I was quiet for a moment as I processed what I heard. Then feeling as if I was going to burst, I said, "I'm sorry but I don't agree with that. I don't think that we should invite them [the rabbi and imam] as a *token* in order to be politically correct but really not value them. I don't see it that way at all. I feel that the participation of other faith traditions will enrich the program." I'm sure there were others who felt the same way, but no one else spoke up. At any rate, no one challenged me.

It is not only Christians who can practice religious bigotry. This underlying attitude toward other people's beliefs can be found in every religion. Most often it is kept hidden, harming the person who thinks that way more than anyone else. If you believe that your way, your beliefs, is the only way, and that everyone else is either wrong or misinformed, in addition to the ill will you create, you cut yourself off from the spiritual riches and wisdom that other faith traditions have to offer.

In my job as chaplain, I work with many people, including religious leaders from several different faiths. If I am welcomed to pray with someone who is Jewish, whether it is a Psalm or some specific prayer from his or her tradition, or with a person who practices Islam, I am honored and humbled and consider myself tremendously blessed by the experience.

In my heart there is no barrier between me and another person who is reaching out for God's healing and peace within the context of his or her own religious tradition. I have found that I do not have to know everything about a particular religion to be welcomed by a person who practices it. I just have to convey that I respect and honor it. Honoring, respecting, and welcoming other people and their beliefs into my life is the key that has opened many doors for me with people, and provided a wealth of spiritual growth as well.

CONNECTING POINT

Today, consider how you really feel about religions other than your own. Do other religious beliefs have anything to offer that can enrich your life?

PRAYER

Lord, help me to live in your world free from the divisiveness that religion can create. Instead, help me to realize that other people's beliefs lead them to you as the beliefs that I hold dear lead me. Grant that I never tread upon another's dreams or beliefs. Amen.

28 Bitter or better?

suffering and the human journey

▶ CHARLES W. SIDOTI

Everyone experiences suffering. It is how we choose to live with it that makes the difference. In May 2004, I attended a professional seminar at Metro Health Medical Center in Cleveland. The topic of the seminar was "Suffering and the Human Journey." One of the speakers, Kathleen Brehony, PhD, left an impression that I will never forget.

The first slide of Dr. Brehony's presentation and her explanation of it captivated me. On the slide appeared the question "Better or Bitter?" Dr. Brehony began by making the observation that everyone suffers; we all have hard times in life, experience losses, encounter illness and eventually death. She presented the observation that some people come through suffering "better," meaning the experience made them more human, more compassionate toward others and themselves, with an increased sense of gratitude, connectedness, and hope. Others, however, come out of suffering "bitter," more resentful and angry, feeling isolated and hopeless.

What accounts for the difference?

This was the first time I had heard the issue put this way, but my many years as a hospital chaplain have confirmed the truth of her observation. Suffering affects people differently. Some are made *better*; they grow and "open up" from the experience. For others, suffering just seems to increase their bitterness, causing them to further close in upon themselves and increasingly shut others out.

As I began to reflect on this concept, I realized it had tremendous implications for both my personal life and my work as a chaplain. I have come to realize that the way each of us will respond to suffering when it comes is largely determined by how "open or closed" we are in our daily lives. If we are able to see life as a continual process of growth, if we can live in such a way that we are open to change within ourselves and within our relationships with others, we will be better positioned to grow through the natural suffering that comes our way. On the other hand, I've come to realize that if we are closed, living in our own little world, preoccupied with getting what we want for our own families and ourselves, the more likely we are to become bitter, closing our fists even tighter when suffering comes to us.

Someone once made the following observation. "We have all met the old man or woman who, although they may have had a hard life, still have a twinkle in their eye and a smile on their face, and that attracts people to them. On the other hand, we have also met the kind of old man or woman, who, when talking, are always complaining. If it is not their health, aches, and pains, it's how terrible the world is becoming. Nothing and no one is any good anymore. Individuals like this do not attract us and we tend to be looking at our watch when we are with them."

The point I want to convey here is that we do not become the old person with the twinkle in the eye, or the bitter old person, overnight. We take a step toward becoming one or the other every day.

The key to growing through our suffering will be our ability to remain open to growth and possibilities during the difficult times in our life. "Suffering can be the force that knocks out our illusionary beliefs about life and thrusts us toward a new consciousness about ourselves and the true nature of life." It is often mentioned during seminars and presentations that the Chinese symbol for the word "crisis" is actually a combination of the symbols for two other words. The first word is "danger" and the second is "opportunity." This is a wonderful way to view the difficult times in our life. If we truly believe that the opportunity for growth is a real part of our crises (our suffering), that belief will help us to be open to the possibility of growth, healing, and new life offered to us in the very midst of that suffering. Realizing that hidden within our times of personal crisis and suffering is the opportunity for personal and spiritual growth changes our outlook in a meaningful and positive way.

CONNECTING POINT

Strive to remain open to possibilities. During times of personal suffering, talk with someone you trust and respect. Very often another person's opinion, because it comes from an objective perspective, can be very helpful in directing you to see the opportunity for growth that you might not be able to see in the midst of your struggle.

PRAYER

Lord, help me to be and to remain open to your guidance in times of suffering, whether that guidance comes from you speaking to me within my own heart or through the voice of another person you have placed in my life to counsel me. Let me not become so discouraged in my struggles that I close myself off from the life process and from you. Help me to remember that I never really face my suffering alone, although at times it indeed feels that way. Awaken me to your presence and help me to open my heart to you. Amen.

29 Slow down... let life catch up!

▶ CHARLES W. SIDOTI

Worry is a way of mentally living the future today. There is nothing inherently wrong with imagining what the future will bring. We do this all the time. One example is when we are lost in thought, projecting with our mind's eye about some future positive event. This is a pleasant experience we call daydreaming.

Worry is different. To worry is to engage in the same mental activity as daydreaming but with one fundamental difference. The future event we are projecting is negative and fearful instead of pleasant. When someone is daydreaming, we sometimes refer to him or her as having drifted off into a daydream. The implication is that the person is relaxed and is lulled into this pleasant experience. The opposite is true of worry. As you begin to worry, your mind speeds up trying desperately to resolve something that you presume will be a problem in the future. The end result is frustration and pain, because your mind is powerless to penetrate the future, which is where the resolution to your perceived problem will eventually be lived out.

The Twenty-Third Psalm provides some wonderful guidance in this regard for anyone who desires to move from being a worried, fearful person to living a more peaceful life. It does this by helping us learn to allow ourselves to be led. Recall the message found in Reflection Sixteen, "Like a Shepherd"; the most powerful phrase of this psalm comes at the very beginning: "The Lord is my shepherd." These simple but powerful words can help us to turn our hearts and minds toward God. They can slow us down, reminding us that there is a higher power at work in our lives. Saying "The Lord is my shepherd" with all the sincerity you can muster at a difficult time, will remind you to wait on the Lord as whatever situation you are facing evolves. When our mind is racing, we are mentally moving faster than life is unfolding. If we are able to realize this, we can decide to slow down our mind and allow life to catch up. Recall from the introduction that God's time is different from our time. At some point it will be necessary for you to decide that you will allow yourself to be led as life slowly unfolds, and then respond to what unfolds. This is a different way of living, a way that abandons the habit of worry.

Equally important to slowing down our mind is opening up our heart to the life process in order to be receptive to God's guidance coming from within our ever-changing lives. When we are worried it is as though we are wearing mental blinders, much like the blinders that block out a racehorse's peripheral vision. We are tense and very focused on making happen what we think needs to happen. We are not open to receive what life offers us as it unfolds.

We need to acquire a taste for allowing our problems to be resolved in the living out of life, instead of trying to resolve them in our imagination through attempts to predict the future by worrying about it. This will mean making a decision not to worry when tempted to do so, and see what happens. Start small. The next time some worry or concern presents itself, try saying in your mind and heart, "The Lord is my shepherd." This little spiritual exercise can help you get in touch, if only for a moment, with the higher power that is at work within your life. It can help you make a spiritual connection.

CONNECTING POINT

Recognize when your thoughts begin to race with a worrisome thought. Consciously decide to slow down your mind and let life's unfolding events catch up to your racing thoughts. As often as you do this, you will find God is there—in the unfolding. Remember, as explained in Reflection Sixteen, that when you say the words "The Lord is my shepherd," you are really saying, "I trust you, God."

PRAYER

God who is, who was, and is to come, help me to slow down that I may grow in awareness of your gentle presence in the daily unfolding of my life. When I am tempted to enter into worry, help me to allow you to lead me and to acknowledge that you, Lord, are my shepherd. Amen.

30 Let go of the mouse

an antidote for control freaks

▶ RABBI AKIVA FEINSTEIN

Obeying Microsoft's recommendations can lead to catastrophe. That's what happened to me when I innocently clicked on "Yes" in the window that recommended condensing my e-mails in order to save space on my hard disk. Some twenty minutes later, the job was done—and my last month and a half of e-mails had disappeared.

"Don't panic," I told myself. "They must be in there somewhere." But as the thought of dozens of red-flagged e-mails that needed urgent replies began to haunt me, I became increasingly agitated. A frantic forty-five seconds later, I called Microsoft's technical support, at who knows what cost per hour, hoping for anything to get me out of this.

The support person was reassuring. "Don't worry," he calmed me. "They're in there somewhere."

"So what do I do?" I asked, almost out of breath.

"Well, it's a little complicated," he said. "I don't think you'll be able to do it on your own. Are you willing to share control of your computer with me until we solve the problem?"

A person drowning in cyberspace will agree to anything. "Yes. Yes!" I promised.

The first thing he had me do was download the program "Microsoft Easy Assist." Then a window appeared, asking if I was willing to share control of my computer with a Microsoft technical support assistant. "Yes," I clicked emphatically.

A small blue box appeared in the lower right-hand corner of my screen. It asked the same question again. Apparently, relinquishing control is not so easy for some people. "It's okay," I told him on the phone. "I trust you." I clicked "Yes," and the little blue box switched messages. Now it assured me that at any time I wanted to withdraw control from the technical support assistant, all I had to do was click the appropriate box. "Why would I want to do that?" I wondered. "He's helping me do what I could never do by myself. I guess some people really have control issues."

"Okay, are you ready?" he asked.

"Yes."

"Now, let go of the mouse."

"Excuse me?"

"Let go of the mouse. I'm going to control your mouse."

What? Who is going to control my computer?

"If you want me to restore your e-mails," he explained patiently, "you have to let me control your mouse." I let go.

Then, like some preternatural Ouija board, my pointer started to move by itself. With my hands tightly folded on my lap and my eyes wide, I saw the pointer moving rapidly and clicking. I was doing nothing. He was doing everything.

Ten minutes later, the phantom e-mails were sitting back in my Outlook Express. I was told to click on the little blue box, withdrawing permission for him to control my computer. I did so reluctantly. Obviously, he knew how to run my computer better than I did.

While some of us are worse control freaks than others, all of us resist relinquishing control of our lives to God. We human beings have been in competition with the Almighty ever since Adam and Eve were seduced into eating the fruit of the Tree of Knowledge by the enticement: "You will become like gods." We so badly want to control our own fate, but at the same time, we are terribly afraid of what will happen if we really are in control and no one is helping us.

What's wrong with wanting to control your own life rather than letting God be God? First of all, thinking that you are in ultimate control of everything that happens to you is extremely stressful. It is obvious that we are put here in this world that is full of challenges to our faith and our trust, to our morals, and to just about everything else. God wants a lot from us in this world, expecting us to do a lot more than we think that we can. But there is no need to go making a challenge where there simply is none. The fact is that there are many areas in our life that are just so confusing, complicated, and downright messy that if we were to get involved, we would only make things worse.

So then, why are they there? What is an appropriate way of responding to difficult life situations that involve things outside our control? It is important to realize that sometimes for us, *not doing* is actually doing. If I am presented with a difficult challenge, and I respond by admitting to myself that I cannot handle the problem alone and give up trying to do so by entrusting the matter to God, I am really doing something extremely meaningful by *not doing* anything. In my thought and even in my action (inaction), I am showing a profound understanding of the way God made the universe. This universe is a partnership between God and us. God does and we do. I am to do what I do well and God does what God does well. I am good at loving my children, going to synagogue, being a good person, going to work. But God's work is different from my work. This is so because God occupies a very different position from us in our lives and in the universe, with abilities far beyond anything we can imagine.

With my messed-up computer representing my life, and the support person representing God, my encounter with the computer support technician provides a compelling analogy to the way in which God is present in our lives. In both situations, I am faced with an issue or problem that is far beyond my ability to solve, and I clearly need help. In both situations, in order to receive that help, I must ultimately relinquish my control and put my trust in the action, knowledge, and wisdom of the "other." In both situations, the help (and helper) comes to us from *within* the mess—the computer, our lives.

So how do we put the wisdom of this analogy to work in our everyday life? First, realize that it is not a matter of having to reach a point of total frustration after first trying to solve life's problems before finally throwing up our hands in complete despair saying, "Okay, it's God's turn now." This may work for a while, but how long can you do it? This is no way to live. Our life becomes much simpler when we learn how to determine from the very beginning, as soon as the challenge presents itself, if the issue is something we can resolve with our own God-given abilities or not.

The point is that to make this determination, we need to talk to God about whatever we may be facing. If it seems that you can handle a particular problem, great. Ask God to guide and bless you with the ability to do what *you* need to do. If you decide that the problem involves issues that are outside your control, admit to yourself and to God that you just don't have what it takes, and ask God to take over. This is where relinquishing control comes in and where peace is found.

It was amazing to watch the mouse, remotely controlled by a support technician, moving on my computer screen solving my computer's woes. It is infinitely more amazing and wonderful to see, at the heart of whatever challenges or changes I am presently experiencing, the hand of God mysteriously and lovingly moving within the context of my life.

CONNECTING POINT

Being "stressed out" as it relates to the fast pace of modern life is a very popular topic of conversation today. Part of the reason for our stressed-out feelings is that it is difficult to let go of the idea that we need to do everything. We should often recall the fact that God already knows how to run this universe. Responding with trust to a difficult challenge by relinquishing our control when the situation calls for it, we are not giving up on life but demonstrating an understanding of how the universe works. Part of personal and spiritual growth involves the realization that the great challenge of living resides not in us *doing everything* but rather in knowing when to step back from our constant doing long enough to allow God to do God's part without our interference.

PRAYER

Dear Lord, you really know how to run this world and what it is that I need to do to perform my part well. Please strengthen me to do that which you intend to complete and enlighten me, and then give me faith to trust in you to do the rest. After all is said and done, grant me the peace of mind to know that I have done all that I can do, and that I have believed in you as much as I could, whether the work is completed or not. Help me to wait in hope for your promise to be fulfilled in my life and in this world. Amen.

31 The irony and inconsistency of grief

▶ RABBI AKIVA FEINSTEIN
and CHARLES W. SIDOTI

Have patience with everything unresolved in your heart.
Don't scratch for answers that cannot be given now. The
point is to try to live everything. Live the questions for now.
Perhaps then, someday far into the future, you will gradu-
ally, without even noticing it, live your way into the answer.
– RAINER MARIA RILKE (GERMAN-LANGUAGE POET)

When life turns difficult, a common way of trying to get around
the pain is to try to think our way out of the situation. The problem with this is that it assumes the process of effectively dealing
with emotional upset and spiritual challenges is linear, sort of like
a Betty Crocker recipe, in that one step necessarily follows another
in order to get the desired outcome. The truth is that the process
of inner healing is inherently non-linear and is often contradictory.
When things do get better and our inner struggle eases for a while,

we often don't know how or why we feel better, we just do. Have you ever gone to sleep with a problem on your mind and awakened not troubled by it anymore? As the saying goes, "What a difference a day makes!" Nothing about your problem changed, you just went to sleep.

Our mood and therefore our perspective change constantly, and that has much to do with the way we process the problems that come our way. Sometimes we wake up feeling great and ready to face the day's challenges. On these days, problems that come up don't bother us too much. We process them easily because we approach them from a positive perspective and keep moving along. The very next day (or even hour), we may feel totally different. The world seems to be spinning in the wrong direction and it seems that everyone is working against us. In addition to affecting the way we handle the daily problems that arise, our moods and our perspective affect the way we handle the big problems in our lives. This is especially true regarding the way we process grief, the pain involved in losing someone or something very important to us.

The Jewish tradition, which is full of wisdom gained by facing pain and suffering head-on, says a great deal about mourning, and how to understand the life path and grief process of the mourner. Mourners often suffer deep anguish and trauma; and helping them to recover, according to Jewish tradition, requires the implementation of customs and practices that can seem contradictory. Yet these work well in helping mourners deal with their own contradictory feelings. For example, individual mourners can feel the need both to be alone and to be surrounded by people and love; the need for silence, and the need to be able to tell their story; the need to give and the need to receive; they can experience waves of denial and waves of acceptance. It's contradictory, yes, but it all can be a very real and necessary part of the healing process and the nature of mourning. It is very wise counsel to advise a mourner thus: "Let these contradictory feelings be, feel what you feel. Live with the contradiction and don't fight it, for it will eventually evolve into something else."

It is very difficult to put this advice into practice, for in our rational, modern society, we find these contradictory truths difficult to accept. The fact is that the suggestion to learn to live with contradiction is not just some remnant of a confused, outdated psychological model. Rather, it's a keen insight into the human condition itself and is a testimony to the power and efficiency of contradiction. For example, human relationships are uniquely able to stay intact despite competing feelings of pure love and absolute frustration. There are rules to human emotion and pain, but the hope and the salvation lie in the fact that for much of it, there are no rules. It is what it is. You can be sad and be happy at the same time. You can harbor a lot of pain, but still move on. You can cherish a memory of a lost dream and still pursue a brand new one.

Quantum physics, which helps us to at least begin to understand the universe, is based upon one of the most poorly understood contradictions known, yet it works and does its job just fine. Quantum physics teaches that it can be scientifically proved that light travels in waves (up and down) but it can also be proved that light moves as physical particles. A person with knowledge of quantum physics understands these principles to be mutually exclusive, yet the whole science of quantum physics is based on both of them being true.

CONNECTING POINT

If we cannot answer life's questions, we should not go into despair. Many a Jewish grandfather would tell his children, "From an unanswered question, you don't die." Living with the questions makes life much more exciting. A life lived looking for something that has not been found yet is a whole lot more interesting. Consciously deciding to *live the questions* is a way of responding with trust to life and its inherent challenges.

PRAYER

God, before whom generations rise and fall, increase in me the ability to live peacefully with the multitude of feelings and emotions that flow in and out of my consciousness. Help me to trust that ultimately it is you who is guiding my life, regardless of what I may feel in a particular moment. Amen.

32 The greater question

▶ RABBI AKIVA FEINSTEIN
and CHARLES W. SIDOTI

Seldom does a week (or even a day or an hour) go by when we are not confronted by the question "Why?" Why are lives devastated by illness and hunger? Why financial crisis, abusive and broken relationships? Why car wrecks and plane crashes? Why do children need to die? Our generation is also challenged by global "whys?" There are catastrophic natural phenomena, tsunamis, earthquakes, war, and events like 9/11, to name but a few. Tragedy eventually leaves its mark on all of us, and it is the cause of much suffering. To each of us, it seems that our own affliction is the most painful.

The modern world is a place of constant searching for answers, and very often answers are found. Yet for this most basic of questions, there is no easy answer. Moses himself asked God, "Why?" and was told, "You will see my back, but my face may not be seen" (Exodus 33:23). This verse has been interpreted to mean that, as humans, we cannot possibly comprehend the events that unfold before our eyes because our lives on earth are but a split second in the evolution of the universe. The span of a human life is simply too brief to achieve any meaningful understanding of the ways of the universe. Just as we cannot judge a movie by arriving in the middle and leaving before the end, we cannot judge God's master plan, for us or for the world. It is only with the passage of significant amounts of time that we could hope to gather even a measure of illumination.

Yes, it is true that some measure of genuine wisdom can, and often does, come with age. However, that wisdom, when it comes, normally teaches us to abandon our personal need to understand *why* things happen. It helps us to allow ourselves to be led by the wisdom of God instead of relying upon our own understanding. With such wisdom the question "Why?" is still present, but it gets integrated into our lives in such a way that we are able to live with it. Its negative power is replaced by trust and the realization that we are not God. It is important to understand that if our only response to something bad occurring is to continually ask "Why?" insisting that we are made to understand the reason why God allowed it to happen, we run the risk of becoming bitter and cynical toward life. It is perfectly natural to ask "Why?" but our response needs to go further if we are to grow spiritually.

It is common in Jewish study to seek clarification on any given subject by returning to the literal meaning of that concept in the Hebrew language. The Hebrew word for suffering is *sevel*. There are two other words that share the very same root, and yet have totally different meanings—*sabal*, porter, and *savlanut*, patience. The connection between these three words became very clear to me (Rabbi Feinstein) one day many years ago, when I was observing the activity at a busy outdoor marketplace in Jerusalem. A merchant finished with his day's selling noticed that he could not carry home his large load of unsold wares and called upon the services of a *sabal*, a porter. To my surprise, I noticed that the porter was not upset at the vast amount of wares that he was being hired to carry. On the contrary, he was delighted. Instead of viewing the large load as a burden and a hard job, he seemed to be saying to himself that the heavier it was, the better, for he could charge a higher price.

It occurred to me then that our own suffering, if we could learn to accept it in some measure into our lives, could serve a similar purpose for us. Even as the *sabal* (the porter), cheerfully carried his heavy load knowing that he would be compensated, we can be buoyed by the knowledge that our *sevel* (our suffering) is not in vain. We can live with confidence that our suffering has a higher purpose and represents an opportunity for growth, even though that purpose and opportunity may not be apparent to us. Another helpful translation is found in the Hebrew word for *crisis*. The word is *mashbir*, which translates into English as birthing stone. This translation suggests that if we can learn to live with patience (in Hebrew, *savlanut*) turning our hearts to God, who is present in the midst of our crisis, new life can come forth.

Crisis always involves something over which we have little or no control. For example, we cannot control the harmful and destructive actions of those who unjustly wage war or terrorize others. We cannot prevent extreme weather or other types of natural disasters from causing terrible devastation around the globe. Our response to crisis is something different: We control and choose how we will respond to these events. Our personal response to suffering is our responsibility, and we do have a choice.

I once heard it said that there is a greater question that presents itself in times of personal suffering and crisis. "Now that this terrible thing has happened, what will my response be?" After asking "Why?" we need to take the next step, asking, "What can I do to ease the suffering of those involved? What is the loving response?"

How we choose to respond to situations is sometimes the only thing that is within our control.

You may be old enough to remember the very popular TV sitcom *All in the Family* from the 1970s. I recently watched a documentary about the making of the show. The producer, Norman Lear, was describing each character and how each personality was an important ingredient in the show's success. When describing Archie Bunker's wife, Edith (Jean Stapleton), who was frequently referred to as a "dingbat," he commented that Edith always responded to a situation from "a place of love." That is indeed a very accurate description of her character, and it provides an example from which we can learn. Edith always responded out of love to whatever the circumstance or crisis. The cynicism of Archie (Carroll O'Connor) was used to rub up against Edith's innocence to create much of the humor of the show, and it worked. Although she was referred to as a dingbat, Edith's loving, honest, and innocent way of responding to situations was always shown to be right in the end. Perhaps she wasn't a dingbat after all.

Edith always responded to situations from a place of love because she was filled with love. But we can, and often do, respond from other places, such as fear, jealousy, blind ambition, or resentment, if our inner space is occupied by any of these. That is why paying attention to what is going on inside us is so important. Whatever occupies our inner space, most of the time, will often be the place from which our responses come. It is important to ask God to help us welcome love, peace, tolerance, acceptance, and a healthy sense of justice into our hearts. In that way our responses to personal crises or the suffering of others will more often be born out of love and compassion. If we learn to pay attention to our inner world, what is going on inside of us, it will be a great help toward our goal of growing into the person God is calling us to become.

Why God allowed this or that to happen will eventually become less important than the greater question, "How is God calling me to respond?"

CONNECTING POINT

Our response to the suffering in this life, whether it be our own suffering or that of others, must involve more than asking the question, "Why?" and insisting on an answer. Suffering is an unpleasant part of life, but it is, nevertheless, a part of life. If we can learn to accept suffering as a mystery in our life, not seeking it out, but rather allowing it to be a part of our experience, God will use it to bring about a newness of life within us. We will discover that, although in a different way from joy and happiness, the suffering that naturally comes our way has its part to play in our spiritual growth and in our becoming the loving person God is calling us to be.

PRAYER

Loving God, help me to welcome your spirit of love, patience, mercy, and kindness into my heart each day, so that I may more often respond out of these virtues to the suffering that I experience in my own life and the suffering that I see in the world. Give me the humility to accept that I may never fully understand the reason why bad things are permitted to happen. Instead of letting me despair over this lack of understanding, help me to place my trust and hope in you who makes all things work for the good of those who love you. Amen.

PART THREE

Relationship with God

The interrelated, fundamental themes "waiting in hope" and "responding with trust" found in the first half of this book are inherently present in the second half. If not specifically mentioned, they are contained within, and are inseparable from, the message of each reflection.

Learning to wait upon the Lord can help us break free of illusions that we may have about who God is, and who we really are. It is key to entering more fully into a lifelong relationship with the Living God. Beginning in childhood and throughout our lives, you and I are presented with many images of God. There is nothing wrong with having an image of God; it is a natural part of our spiritual development. However, if our relationship with God is to be lifelong it must grow and evolve, as we grow and evolve, beyond images, or it will cease to hold meaning for us as adults. It is my hope that the following reflections may inspire and encourage you as you continue to seek God's presence on your own sacred journey.

33 The Living God

a grown-up perspective

▶ CHARLES W. SIDOTI

As a child growing up in a Christian family, I had a belief in Santa Claus that was a fun and exciting part of the Christmas holiday. When I had children of my own, I enjoyed seeing the excitement on their faces as they heard the story of the magical jolly fellow who lived at the North Pole and delivered gifts on Christmas Eve to all of the good little children. All this he did while riding on his magic sleigh with eight tiny reindeer! What could be better? One day my eight-year-old son, Charles, and I were taking a walk with our dog when he asked me, "Is God like Santa Claus?" I had to pause for a moment. The last thing I wanted to do was explain away the wonderful childhood fantasy of Santa Claus for him.

The reasoning that led Charles to ask this question is very easy to understand. To him, it seemed completely logical that God should exist in exactly the same way as a character like Santa Claus. Think about it. A child never actually sees Santa, although children do see Santa's "helpers" at the department store. Children are told that Santa Claus lives at the North Pole and keeps a close eye on kids' behavior, rewarding the ones who are good and disappointing the ones who are bad. At roughly the same age that children are told about Santa, they also begin learning about God. To a child, God is also explained as someone with seemingly magical powers. Children are told that God is watching over us from heaven, a place that seems as remote as the North Pole. They learn that God is also someone who cares about them, knows everything about them, and wants them to be good. Children learn that God's helpers are called angels, who are all around but never seen. Santa's workers are called "elves," and we can't see them, either! And just as with Santa, we never see God. It is little wonder why Charles asked me if God was the same as Santa.

At some point, we need to grow beyond a child's understanding of God. Our relationship with God must grow and evolve with us into adulthood or it will cease to contain meaning, just like our relationship with Santa. Every meaningful relationship grows and changes or it simply dissolves. Our relationship with our parents is a good example. A small child sees his or her parents as all-knowing, all-powerful beings. If our relationship with our parents is a healthy one, it evolves as we grow into adulthood. It is then that we are able to see and appreciate our parents for what they really are, human beings.

What determines if a relationship grows or ends? The difference is communication. With Santa there is no real two-way communication, because there is no real Santa. With God it is different. Growing in the awareness of God's presence in our life and becoming aware of God's constant communication are what is meant by learning to live a *contemplative* life. For our relationship with God to be meaningful and real as adults, we need this awareness of God's presence and recognition of the many ways God communicates with us. The transition from believing in a magical, Santa-like God to growing in relationship with the Living God happens in ways that are as individual as we are. Each person's relationship with God is different. Personally, my exposure to the monastic tradition, especially the writings of Thomas Merton and other contemplative authors, has had a profound impact on my own spiritual development.

One of the greatest gifts that the monastic tradition can bestow upon a person is what I refer to as the development of a contemplative mindset. By a contemplative mindset, I am referring to the realization that God comes to us from within creation, indeed from within our very selves. God isn't "up there" somewhere, removed from this world. God is present within the context, the events, of our everyday lives. It is within the events of our everyday life that God desires to meet us, guide us and heal us. The awareness that all of life is sacred, that all of God's creation is good and the place where God dwells, is a profoundly healing realization. It is the fruit of attentively waiting upon the Lord through the events and circumstances of our lives. When you see God in this way, it is impossible to think of God as a Santa Claus figure, somewhere far removed from us and looking down. No, God is very close, indeed an in-dwelling presence.

CONNECTING POINT

Your image, the way you think of (or see) God, should grow and evolve as you journey through life. Do you think yours has? Ask God in your own words to place in your heart the desire to grow in that relationship.

PRAYER

Lord, help me to grow in relationship with you, the "Living God." Direct my heart that I may wait patiently upon you to reveal yourself to me. May I become increasingly aware of the many ways that you communicate your love and presence to me every day, and may I respond sincerely through my life with others and in the solitude of prayer. Amen.

34 In the midst of change

God comes to us
from within creation

▶ CHARLES W. SIDOTI

Your awareness of God's presence will increase as you learn to better accept and process change in your life. Perhaps the reason so much has been said and written about how to deal with life's constant change is because coming to terms with it is so important to anyone who desires to know inner peace. I once heard author Joan Frances Guntzelman, PhD, speak at a professional chaplains' seminar in Columbus, Ohio. She talked about the constant change so present in our lives in a most interesting way. Guntzelman made the observation that "there is a pattern to the universe, of life, death and rebirth." She emphasized that even though we can, and often do, struggle against it, the pattern remains.

There is an important lesson here, one that connects well with the thought of the ancient Greek philosopher Heraclites, who made the observation that "you cannot step into the same river twice." This statement is both profound and absolutely true. Imagine yourself sitting on a riverbank with your foot dangling in the flowing water. In the split second it takes you to pull your foot out and put it back into the water, the whole river has changed. It is always on the move. And so it is with all of life.

I have come to realize that the longer we live, the more we will observe that the things that "today" fill up our life and provide its meaning are changing, or will eventually go away altogether: children, work, family, and friends. The crucial thing for us to realize is that while something is always dying, there is always something being born. We need to learn to wait to see what is being born. It is worth noting that most major religions refer to the pattern of life, death, and rebirth, and invite one to "enter in" according to the group's belief system and traditions. The pattern is found throughout nature. The caterpillar's transformation into a butterfly is one of the countless examples.

It is important to realize that although the process of continuous change that is found in the universe can be difficult for us to accept, it is not negative. In fact, it is the opposite of negative. There is a real sense in which it is appropriate to say that without death, without the constant change that occurs, there can be "no life."

In the film *Groundhog Day*, the main character was caught in an endless cycle in which he was literally reliving the same day over and over again. At first, it was comical to watch, as he was able to predict what was going to occur each day because absolutely nothing had changed from the previous day. He just moved through the day as the same people and situations repeated themselves to his amusement. As the story continued, with nothing changing in his life, the man became extremely depressed. The story stopped being funny, taking on a darker tone than one might expect to find in a comedy film. The character was able to finally break free of the terrible cycle by *choosing* to change the *way* he spent his day. The film provided a fictional but poignant example of what life would be like if nothing changed. It was not a pretty sight.

During a homily at the Church of the Holy Angels, the church that I attend, Fr. Dan Schlegel gave one of the best insights I've ever heard about how change, while difficult, is an extremely positive force in our lives. He told the story of his first Mass at a new parish. An elderly woman had approached him after the Mass and begun to talk about how much the Catholic Church had changed. She went on and on about how things used to be. As she talked, Father Dan recalled to us, he was mentally preparing himself to hear how terrible she thought all the changes were. To his surprise, she ended by saying, "But it's the changes that keep us alive, isn't it!" Father Dan explained that he was pleasantly surprised and encouraged, and learned something from his encounter with that woman.

As we learn to accept the continual change that is so much a part of our lives, we will, to a greater extent, come to know the Living God, who is present in the very midst of every change that we experience. God is to be found in the very heart of our struggles, our joys, and our relationships. God comes to us from within creation, within other people, and indeed within our very selves!

CONNECTING POINT

Change is not the enemy. It simply means you are alive. Change is the way God's work is revealed in your life. Have you ever looked back upon a time of significant change in your life, possibly a time when you felt you were facing a situation alone, and found in hindsight that God's guidance was actually there all the time?

PRAYER

Lord, help me to see your invitation to grow in and through the many changes of my life. Help me to realize that whether the change is one that I welcome, a difficult change, or even a tragic one, I never face it alone. Grant that I may remain open in the midst of the changes that occur, even though I may have to wait a period of time, so that in the midst of them I may discover your presence ready to guide me. Amen.

35 Everyone loves a mystery

allowing our lives to unfold

▶ CHARLES W. SIDOTI

Like it or not, our lives are unfolding mysteries. I say "like it or not" because sometimes it is very hard to let our lives be a mystery. Often, we would much rather know the outcome of things—now. The old Beatles song "Let It Be" has always held special meaning for me. The wisdom of the song's message seems to apply especially well in regard to coming to terms with the realm of mystery in our lives. The question is, "Can you...let it be?"

When we talk about the realm of mystery in our lives, we are talking about everything, and everyone, both in this particular moment and beyond. The realm of mystery in our lives is, in large part, about what the future holds for us and for those we love.

Many people, myself included, enjoy a good mystery. The elements of mystery and surprise make for good reading, storytelling, and movies. In fact, one could argue that without them, the stories, movies, and books we enjoy so much would be boring and bland. It is interesting to observe that the very thing we look for in movies and books to make them worthwhile, the element of mystery, is often perceived as threatening to us when it comes to our

129

own personal future. Mystery, as it unfolds in the life of a character in a movie, can be pure joy and entertainment to us. This is because we have no real stake in the outcome of the story or the fate of the character. Not only do we enjoy the presence of mystery in the movies we watch and the books we read; we are *healed* by it. Perhaps what is so healing about a good mystery novel is that by reading it, by allowing ourselves to be absorbed in the story, we enter a state of being where we accept the element of mystery, or the unknown, in our minds and hearts. Again, because we have no stake in the outcome of the story, we are not threatened by it, yet we still benefit emotionally from its healing effect.

And yet, so much of our actual lives are an unfolding mystery, in that the future is unknown to us. So the question becomes: How can we begin to transfer some of the acceptance we have for the element of mystery in books and movies into our own lives as we face the very real future? The first step is to realize that the same "element of mystery" that adds spice to the things we find entertaining also adds spice to our real lives and makes living worthwhile. The more we allow this truth to be integrated into our life, the more we will be able to let life be a mystery. Learning to see the unknown element of your life (the future) as no longer a threat, but simply as the way life is, will allow you to relax. It will enable you to participate, and to respond more freely, to the unfolding mystery that is the story of your life.

CONNECTING POINT

As the saying goes, "The Lord works in mysterious ways." It is absolutely true. God's ways are mysterious to us because of our inability to see into the future. We do not have God's perspective. Just for today, try to believe that God is doing God's part in your life in ways unknown to you. Believe that, eventually, God's unseen work will be made known to you. Realize, however, that it may only be in hindsight that you are able to see it; and that is something to look forward to!

PRAYER

Lord, it is hard to wait, especially when I feel alone and confused. Help me to respond with enough trust in you to allow some measure of mystery in my life. Help me to learn to live with the uncertainty that is a naturally occurring part of life, as unsettling as it is. In those times, help me to really believe that you are at work in my life in ways yet unknown to me, and to trust in your work on my behalf. Help me to be patient. Amen.

36 A necessary conflict

surrendering to the fact that we are not God

▶ CHARLES W. SIDOTI

Learning to become more relaxed and easygoing in life is a wonderful thing. However, if I hold on too tightly to what I think needs to happen before I can be happy, I find myself in a power struggle with the universe. This power struggle makes it impossible to live a harmonious, peaceful life. Unless something changes, this is how I live. If I were God, if I had ultimate control, there would be no conflict, but I'm not, I don't, and there is.

The conflict, however, can be a good, even necessary, element in our personal growth. If we remain open to what the conflict has to teach us, our inner conflict can lead to a new awareness of who we are and who God is. On the other hand, it can cause us to harden our hearts and close our minds. I often ask myself, "Do I really want peace...or is it that I simply 'want what I want'?"

Nineteenth-century American author and poet Oliver Wendell Holmes made an important point when he said, "The great act of faith is when we finally decide we are not God." This quote captivated me because this is exactly where our conflict needs to lead us. I believe this statement is the hinge on which real transformation, and therefore real inner healing, rests. While none of us consciously thinks of himself or herself as being "God," our attempts to control life, manipulate people or situations, and the thousand other ways we try to force life to go the way we think it should, suggest that at a deep level we believe in our own God-like importance.

The good news is that the more hard-headed and persistent we are in behaving as though we were God, the more frustrated and tired we are likely to become. This can lead us to give up trying to be what we are not, and to finally surrender to the fact that we are not God, and become aware of God's presence in a new way. If we can remain open in the midst of the inner struggle, the struggle itself can help us to change our mind about what life is about, and to take our proper place in the universe. Our personal inner conflict can lead us to experience a radical revision and transformation of our whole mental process.

CONNECTING POINT

When you worry, you are trying to control something that is outside your ability to control. Things outside your control are the things for which God is responsible. Remember, "The great act of faith is when we finally decide we are not God."

PRAYER

Loving God, Creator of the universe, help me to know you as my creator and to respond with trust, accepting my proper place as a part of your creation. Help me to let go of the things that are not my responsibility, those things that are not in my power to control, and to entrust them to you with confidence. Amen.

37 Two paths

we choose our path in the everyday situations of life

▶ CHARLES W. SIDOTI

Once the realization that you are not God takes root in your heart, the challenge becomes one of learning to live your life in a balanced way, between letting things happen and making them happen. The challenge is to develop a rhythm between waiting on the Lord and responding with trust. This is important because both of these inner actions are critical to living a more peaceful life and are key principles in our relationship with God. Learning to move between the two involves timing. It is in the timing that peace will be found. Learning to live in this balance can be one of life's greatest struggles, and at the same time it can be one of the most pivotal and rewarding things we can learn. You will need to be patient with yourself. The way you live, the way you relate to life, and your habit of worrying have developed over many years and are natural for you. Making a change, even a positive change, in your approach to life is not something you can bring about by a sheer act of will. It is something that you can learn to identify, accept, and integrate into your life with God's help.

Sometimes the need to reach out for freedom is only realized after we hit the bottom. This can certainly be true of our inner life and the habit of worrying. When you finally get good and tired of living a life of worry, realizing how exhausted you have become living in this way, you will have arrived at a critical point, a crisis point. Surprisingly, this can be the best thing that has ever happened to you.

Wait a minute: Having a personal breakdown is a good thing? It can be. In many ways, when a person reaches his or her breaking point, that person is standing at the proverbial fork in the road. Either path one chooses represents a form of giving up. One path represents giving up into life, surrendering our imagined complete control. Surrendering into life, we learn to allow for down time in our efforts to make things happen and become comfortable letting things happen for a while. In my experience, I sometimes have discovered that a situation has turned out better than I could have ever imagined precisely because I let things happen, backing away for a while, allowing the natural course of events to play out. In this new way of living, we find rest and gain confidence to continue surrendering into life. We begin to relate to life and others in a new way. In a real sense, we are reborn.

The other path represents a form of giving up by turning away from life. On this path, people also give up their imagined complete control, but they just replace it with another illusion, the belief that they have no control. On this path, people become bitter toward life. Turning away from life, they begin to close themselves off from really experiencing the world and other people. They never really learn to relate to others, nor are they interested, because the effort seems futile. The further a person travels down this path, the more isolated, cynical and depressed he or she becomes. The most complete form of turning away from life is suicide.

When the options are presented in this way, the choice seems obvious. Who wouldn't choose the path that leads to inner peace and harmony over the one that leads to isolation and depression? But it is important to realize that where you are now, sitting and reading this book, is not where your choice will be made, at least not entirely. You and I choose which path we tread in the everyday situations in which we find ourselves, especially in our interactions with others. The challenge, the one thing necessary, is to pray that you may remain open on your life's journey, that you may continue to grow by turning "into" life. The rest will follow, in God's time.

CONNECTING POINT

Giving up or surrendering our imagined sense of control, finding comfort and peace in the higher power of God's real control over our lives, is what giving up into life means.

PRAYER

Loving God, Creator of the universe, in your time help me to let go of my destructive way of relating to life through my worry and a false sense of my ability to control life. Open my heart to a new way of living, a peaceful way of surrender, trusting in your loving presence guiding my life. Amen.

38

Even when I am afraid

trusting during times of inner darkness

▶ CHARLES W. SIDOTI

What do you think it really means to live by faith? Growing in faith is about learning to trust during those times when we cannot see clearly and cannot understand what is happening in our lives. Faith is very much about what we choose to do when we are afraid.

Faith is often referred to as light. Joyce Rupp, in her book *Little Pieces of Light*, reflects on the many different ways in which inner darkness, while not something we find pleasant, is a naturally occurring and even necessary part of our spiritual growth. She makes the point that sometimes the light, compared to the darkness we are experiencing, can seem very tiny.

Rupp tells the story about how she and some others were preparing a room for a retreat they were directing on the topic of Native American Spirituality. They wanted to provide the people attending the retreat with a prayer experience called "the Pipe Ceremony," which begins with an experience of total darkness. The darkness of the specially prepared room would symbolize the womb of Mother Earth from which we all come. To prepare the room for the prayer ceremony, the group closed all the windows and curtains, even putting black plastic bags and tape over all of the cracks around the doors, hoping to block out all outside light. The ceremony began with the group sitting in a circle as the leader turned off the lights.

Rupp describes the moment when the lights were switched off as an "instant flood of blackness—like falling into a black hole." Rupp describes how, as her eyes adjusted to the darkness, she began to see "tiny little pieces of light." These tiny beams of sunlight were penetrating the extremely small holes around the window frames that the tape had not completely covered. She explains how she "smiled deeply inside herself" when she saw those tiny pieces of light through the darkness. In her words, "Yes, I thought, 'this is what has always sustained me in the tough times. No matter how thick the darkness, the light has always remained.' This reality has convinced me that I can live through dark experiences and not be overcome."

As I reflect on my own experiences with inner darkness, I am able to relate to Rupp's description. Rupp shared her experience of needing to let her eyes adjust to the sudden darkness during her retreat experience before she could see the tiny pieces of light. In the same way, when tragedy or something unexpected throws us into sudden spiritual darkness, we need to let our inner eyes adjust to that darkness. This waiting on the tiny pieces of spiritual light is another way we can wait on the Lord in our relationship with God.

Looking back on the difficult periods in my life, the light, tiny though it may have been, has always remained. During my times of inner darkness, it has always come down to my personal choice of deciding to follow that seemingly tiny light of faith, reaching out to God for help and mercy from within my inner darkness. Sometimes this has meant just putting one foot in front of the other until the overwhelming darkness dissipated. It always does—eventually!

We can also choose to turn away from the light in complete despair. That I have also done for brief periods of time. For some, as discussed in the last reflection, this turning away from life continues and is ultimately acted out in suicide. Others simply become bitter and cynical toward life, making themselves and those who live with them miserable.

I like to think of faith as being like the flame of a candle, which by its very nature is fragile. It is always on the verge of being extinguished. Yet, when I have been able to remain open in times of darkness, I have discovered that the flame never goes completely out. At times I have seen it grow awfully dim. But it is still there, a tiny piece of light that guides me through difficult times.

CONNECTING POINT

Sometimes it is necessary to wait in our darkness while our inner eyes adjust to that darkness. It is then that the tiny pieces of God's light and presence can be seen. If you can be patient for just a while and resist the urge to panic when darkness and confusion come upon you, no doubt the fragile but powerful light of faith will emerge out of the darkness to light your path.

PRAYER

Lord, it is hard to wait in darkness. The confusion and uncertainty make me fearful. In these moments, help me to wait for my inner eyes to adjust. Help me to be patient and to wait for you to reveal your presence. Give me the strength and the desire to turn toward the light that you provide, allowing it to guide me. Amen.

39 The mystery of goodness

choosing where to focus our attention

▶ CHARLES W. SIDOTI

Our inner peace is influenced in large part by where we choose to focus our attention. Have you ever wondered why murder mysteries and investigative shows are so popular? Why is it said in the news business that "if it bleeds it leads"? I do not believe most people actually enjoy seeing something bad happen to someone else. It is because there is a certain enticement or glamour to the Mystery of Evil that seems to attract us, and the human heart needs mystery. Something mysterious captivates our interest and engages us. Therefore, mystery is good, and can even be considered a healing element in our lives. Modern news and other types of media rely largely on the Mystery of Evil to capture our attention and it has been proved to work over and over again.

There is another source of mystery present in our lives, and it is every bit as captivating and much more prevalent.

One of the most powerful insights for me is what I call the Mystery of Goodness. I began thinking about this concept while reading a wonderful book by Robert J. Wicks called *Everyday*

140

Simplicity: A Practical Guide to Spiritual Growth. In one section, Wicks is talking about the prevalence of evil in our society, as seen both in the news and entertainment media, and how it can lead to discouragement and pessimism. According to Wicks, "Being pessimistic is in vogue. Being hopeful is not. In the media there seems to be a process going on to support this negative cycle." He goes on to describe an encounter he had with someone about this topic in the following way:

> Once someone said to me, in the spirit of this prevailing negative feeling, "Why is there so much evil in the world?" In response to the discouragement in the voice of this fine, loving man, I replied: "Instead, I find a greater question is, in the midst of all the real evil in the world today, why are there so many good people still performing healing acts?"

I call this the Mystery of Goodness. Wicks' question, "With so much that is wrong in the world, why does there continue to be so much goodness and beauty?" is a powerful statement. The Mystery of Evil is fascinating, but isn't it also fascinating, and healthier, to wonder why there continue to be beautiful mountains, glorious sunsets, interesting animals, and acts of human kindness and virtue that go on every day? Why do these things keep on occurring? Why is there so much goodness in the world? Realizing that this is the greater question has led me to a tremendous and very positive insight about life and the world in which we live.

I recently heard someone say, "If you look for reasons to believe that there is order and wisdom in the universe, you will find many reasons to believe it is so." I realized that it is true. I thought about how every day the sun rises in the east and sets in the west; spring follows winter; a caterpillar goes through a transformation and a butterfly emerges; after the pains of labor a child is born. There are an infinite number of examples. On the other hand, if you look for reasons to support the belief that life is simply a series of random, chaotic events, you will find many reasons to support this statement as well. For example, natural disasters occur that devastate parts of our planet, babies are born with terrible birth defects, young people die, there is senseless killing and horrible cruelty, people suffer terrible loneliness and suffering caused by disease and death.

As a hospital chaplain, I am aware of the great physical, mental, and spiritual suffering that is so often a part of life. I have learned it firsthand, experienced it in the lives of my family and friends, and seen it in our world. The suggestion that we spend some time reflecting on the Mystery of Goodness is not intended to minimize the pain, suffering, and presence of evil that are so obviously a part of life. Nor is it meant to suggest that we should try to "look on the bright side" when confronted by evil. It can, however, inspire hope and serve as a powerful reminder that in the midst of a world where so much is wrong, not everything is wrong, although at times it may certainly seem to be. That reminder can be helpful, providing perspective when we most need it. Choosing or perhaps disciplining ourselves to spend at least some time reflecting on the Mystery of Goodness can remind us that life is not only about one thing. For most people, life is not only about suffering and pain, just as it is not only about joy and happiness. It is a combination of both.

As Scripture teaches us, "For everything there is a season, and a time for every matter under heaven" (Ecclesiastes 3:1). Reflecting on the Mystery of Goodness can serve as a reminder that there are seasons to our lives, and the seasons of our lives will change, just as certainly as the sun will rise in the morning.

CONNECTING POINT

What images are awakened in you by the term the Mystery of Goodness? Do you think there is more goodness or more evil in the world? Why do you think that the negative, the evil, gets so much attention? In what ways are you able to recognize the "seasons" in your life?

PRAYER

God of all creation, inspire my heart that I might be overwhelmed with the Mystery of Goodness so present in the world. Help me to see in a proper perspective the evil that is also present, so that it will not cause me to fall into despair. Help me to see the presence of evil as a reason for me to turn to you for help and guidance in facing the challenges it presents, so that I may respond to it appropriately. Amen.

40 God sees it differently...

thanks be to God!

▶ CHARLES W. SIDOTI

God sees the people that you dislike differently than you do. This is one of the most helpful lessons to learn, because once you accept that God sees things differently, it becomes possible for your vision to expand, and for you to see other people more the way that God sees them. The person who benefits the most from your new way of seeing things is you.

When you or I decide that we don't like someone, we cease to see the potential for good in that person. We lose interest in seeing goodness in that person. If someone I do not like is successful at something, or shares a happy story about his or her life, I may find it difficult to truly share in the joy, and I may feel an underlying resentment within me as I listen to the person. God does not do that. The following story may help to illustrate this.

The city where my family and I live, Aurora, Ohio, has been home to Geauga Lake Amusement Park for the past 119 years. Our home is within walking distance of the park. We have purchased season passes to the park every summer since moving to Aurora in 1994. Living so close to the park has been a great summertime experience for our children and a blessing for our whole family. Even when I was a child myself, my family would often go to Geauga Lake. I have very fond childhood memories associated with going there.

At the end of the 2007 season, the owners of Geauga Lake announced that the park was closing due to years of declining attendance. The news was sad to hear. When the local paper printed an article about the park closing, several local people were interviewed, each sharing their personal memories of Geauga Lake. The recollections were interesting to read and made me nostalgic, especially since I could relate to their stories.

As I read further into the article, one of the people interviewed was a local politician, someone I had always found irritating. As I read about the fond memories that he and his family had of Geauga Lake, I felt somewhat annoyed. It wasn't a big deal, but there was a certain reaction in me, and I found that I really did not want to hear *his* story in the middle of my pleasant, nostalgic thoughts about Geauga Lake. Most of us have an unspoken assumption, which just seems to come with being human, that God is automatically on our side in our judgment of others. I was surprised to read this man's story about a happy time in *his* life. "What is this? God is good to *him*, too?"

There are many instances in Scripture where people complain to God about others they perceive to be wicked or undeserving of good things. Those who do the complaining are surprised and annoyed when they see that particular person blessed with good fortune. The story of the prodigal son's brother is one example. Another example from Scripture is the story of the laborers in the vineyard. Some laborers were hired to work early in the morning, some at midday, and others shortly before quitting time, yet they all received the same pay! Those hired early were not pleased.

The fact of the matter is that God sees things differently than you and I do. As quoted earlier, Oliver Wendell Holmes said, "The great act of faith is when we finally decide we are not God." To realize that God sees other people differently from the way we do is to integrate Holmes' wisdom at a very practical level. It makes a difference in the way we live among others because it changes the way we see them. Realizing that God sees people differently can allow us to give others the benefit of the doubt by providing us with a good reason to do so. As you gradually become less judgmental of others, you are the one who will benefit the most, because you will find that you are happier and more peaceful inside.

You may ask, "Does this mean that I need to like everyone?" No, your liking or disliking of certain people may or may not change, and that's okay. The local politician I spoke of still tends to annoy me, but my opinion of him has softened. Realizing that God sees people differently from the way you do can help open you up to a new way of seeing others, which in turn can increase the amount of inner peace in your life.

CONNECTING POINT

Realize that your thoughts about others do not represent God's thoughts. Your opinion of them is not God's opinion. God sees potential for goodness where we are not able to see it. Ask God to help you soften your judgment of others, realizing that God is not finished with them yet, just as God is not finished with you.

PRAYER

Help me, Lord, to grow to see the actions of other people more the way that you do. It is so easy for me to be judgmental. Help me to remember that my sense of righteousness is really self-righteousness when I assume that you see things the way I do. Help me to remember that we are all your children; even the person I don't like is a child of God; and you desire goodness and healing for that person every bit as much as you do for me. I realize that I cannot bring about this change on my own, and wait in joyful hope for you to change my heart. Amen.

41 **Reconnecting**

returning to your spiritual center

▶ CHARLES W. SIDOTI

Everyone's spiritual path is unique, taking us to many different places throughout our lives. It can be extremely helpful to reflect upon your own spiritual road and where it has taken you thus far. One of the special places that my path has taken me has remained a part of my life for many years. Since 1982, I have made an annual monastic retreat at the Abbey of the Genesee, a Trappist monastery in Upstate New York. Exposure to the monastic tradition, especially the writings of Thomas Merton and other contemplative authors, has had a profound impact on my own spiritual development. The Abbey, because of its powerful impact upon my life, is the place I have long considered my spiritual home. I always return there when I need to step away from the events and people in my life to regain perspective. It is a place where I am able to "Be still and know that God is God."

I remember my first trip to the Abbey and listening to Br. Anthony Weber, the guest master at that time, give a lecture to those of us on retreat. It was the opening conference, and Brother Anthony was talking about why it is beneficial to make an occasional personal retreat, why it is good to go away to a quiet place and pray on a regular basis. He used the image of an artist painting

148

a picture and mentioned how at some point during her work, the artist will need to step back from the canvas to look at the overall painting she is creating. This stepping back, or stepping away, is necessary for the artist to gain perspective and to reconnect with the original inspiration behind the work of art. An artist with her nose to the canvas, focused on the details, can lose touch with the original idea behind what she is creating. Likewise, in our personal lives, we can become lost in the details. There is a need to step back to a quiet place, whether it is a weekend retreat or just five minutes a day in a prayer corner of your room. This time away will help you to regain a healthy perspective toward your life and to mentally reconnect with the presence of God in your life.

The last time I visited the Abbey, I discovered a way to bring a small piece of the experience home with me. The Abbey's retreat house and the monastery where services are held are about a mile apart, and walking this mile in solitude is a wonderful part of the retreat experience. The last time I was doing so, I decided to pick up a small rock to take home with me. The stone, less than the size of a quarter, was small enough to fit easily in my pocket.

I carry it with me throughout the day and find myself reaching for it whenever I feel stressed or when things aren't going the way I think they should. As I hold the rock in my hand, it reminds me that there is more going on in my life than what I am able to see and comprehend. It reminds me that there is a larger aspect to life, one in which my life fits, and has importance, and yet is only a part. Touching the rock helps me to remember that I am connected to something greater than myself. This remembering helps me to let go of my compulsive thoughts, even if just for a little while. It helps me to wait on the Lord and to allow God space in my life.

CONNECTING POINT

Is there a special place from your past or present, a place that helps you to feel spiritually centered? It does not need to be a church, temple, or mosque. It might be a place in nature, a lake or woods, any place that is special to you and helps you to refocus. Know that this place, and the peace it provides you, also exist in your heart. In the midst of your daily life find your own way to reconnect with that special place and receive its peace.

PRAYER

Lord, instill in my heart the desire to step back from all of the activity and effort that I put into my life. Help me to make time to reconnect with you. After all, it is you who created me, and you who fills the universe. Help me to see my life and my desires in the proper perspective. Amen.

42 Already one

we are connected to all of creation

▶ CHARLES W. SIDOTI

Life can be very lonely at times. It is also true, however, that we are never really alone. Something common to many religions is that they have certain men and women whose lives of faith stand out in such a way that they serve as examples for others. Some religions call them saints, while other religions do not, but most have their great men and women whose lives inspire others who read or hear about them. There are also people found in many faith traditions whose life stories are well-known and studied by the faithful even though their particular faith group does not officially declare them saints. These may be authors, speakers, clergy or lay people. They may simply be caring, courageous people whose life stories become known and serve to lead others on their own spiritual journey. There are people we have known personally, living and deceased, including family members, friends, coworkers, and acquaintances, who have helped and taught us in the way of faith. The point is that the lives of others, the famous and well-known as well as those in our everyday lives, touch and influence us in deep and meaningful ways.

One of the things I find most beautiful about the Catholic faith is the belief in what is called the "Communion of Saints." While I am not a theologian, I will simply share with you what the teaching means to me, and how I integrate this belief into my own spiritual life. The beauty of the Communion of Saints is that it serves to remind us of our basic connectedness to one another as human beings. The Communion of Saints, however, goes a step further by saying that this connectedness is not bound or limited by the power of death. The wonderful message of this teaching is that our love and unconditional regard for one another transcend space, time, and even death.

This personal story describes how I found comfort in this teaching in my own life. One day I was sitting in the hospital chapel, praying about something that was worrying me. As I sat there, feeling kind of sorry for myself, I began thinking about the lives of such well-known biblical figures as Moses and Abraham. It occurred to me that they, too, had to live their lives by faith, just like me.

We tend to see such biblical figures as larger than life and living with some mysterious advantage that we don't have. We don't see them as having the human limitations with which we live. When we fail to see them as regular people, we limit how helpful their lives and stories can be to us. We sometimes see them as having an inside track to God, kind of like having "the God card" hidden in their back pocket to use when they need it. In reading about them in the Scriptures, it can seem like God broke through the clouds during their times of crisis to speak with them directly, giving them just the advice they needed. We ignore the fact that God has ways of speaking to us, too, offering the same grace, and that what really set these biblical heroes apart is how receptive they were to God's message.

The value in the biblical people we look up to is that they were human, that they had to walk in our shoes, really walk our path. The realization that living a life of faith was just as challenging for them as it is for me caused me to feel a connectedness with them. I found myself calling upon "their faith" to come into my being. I literally said these words in a prayer, "Faith of Abraham and Moses, come unto me. Faith of Mary and Joseph, come unto me." I immediately felt a connection that was both consoling and comforting and that has remained with me. It is a peace that transcends time and space and the separation of religions, a spiritual connection.

Many people, myself included, feel a connection with loved ones or special people who have gone on before us in death. There is a knowledge that comes to us, helping us to know that the love and guidance we enjoyed with these special people did not end with death. Because of physical death, however, the way we experience the relationship changes.

It is not uncommon when talking with people to hear them say that their deceased loved ones live on in their hearts. In our daily lives we help, console, comfort, and pray for one another all the time. The teaching on the Communion of Saints acknowledges that the bonds of love, support, and connectedness we have with others in this life are not limited in any way. The teaching on the Communion of Saints brings to our conscious awareness that in a transcendent yet very meaningful way, we are all connected. We are already one.

CONNECTING POINT

Is there a person, living or dead, whose life of faith you admire? Or is there someone whose life has been a source of wisdom and guidance that has provided you with direction? Realize and take comfort in knowing that they, like you, had to truly live their life by faith. They had no special assistance from God that is not made available to you according to the unique circumstances of your life. Know that the God they prayed to is the same God that hears your prayer today.

PRAYER

God of all the holy men and women who have ever lived, help me to realize that love never dies. Help me to feel connected with you and all of your children. Help me to live in the awareness of the bond of love that exists between you and all people. Help me to know in my heart that we are already one. Amen.

43 **Joy**

a side effect of spiritual growth

▶ RABBI AKIVA FEINSTEIN
and CHARLES W. SIDOTI

"Because you did not serve your God, amid gladness and goodness of heart, when everything was abundant...."

– DEUTERONOMY 28:47

This Scripture verse is truly perplexing. It implies that even if a person is following the commandments and therefore listening to what God wants from him or her, it is still not quite enough. Rather, there is a necessity to serve with joy or otherwise be denied the full blessings of one's actions. All this can seem a bit demanding. Consider that this verse is addressed to God-fearing, religiously observant people, who are seemingly doing all the right things. Is the mere fact that they do not exhibit enthusiasm and joy a reason to punish them?

First of all, it is important to realize that the verse is not about punishment. Rather it is intended to direct us in our journey of spiritual growth to a new awareness about life and about God that

155

is indeed very good. It is an invitation to a fuller, richer, and more abundant way (life with God) than we ever imagined possible.

At the heart of this Scripture is the truth that there is a difference between knowing about God and knowing God. For example, we can know things intellectually about God, or have opinions about God, and yet still not know God. Many of us learned about God as children, either at home or at church or synagogue. We may learn things about God from reading the Bible or other spiritual books that make us think about God. We may also participate in activities that we dedicate to God, such as religious observances, prayer, feeding the poor, attending to the sick, or other acts of charity. But in the end, all these things (by themselves) simply make us religious. And it is quite possible to be very religious and still have no relationship with the Living God from whom comes real joy. This does not mean that religion or religious acts are bad or do not potentially have meaning. It means that they are not enough. Religious acts are meant to lead to something more. If we are open to receiving the goodness that religion has to offer, it will help us to connect spiritually with the world within and around us.

Some definitions

Religion commonly pertains to the way a group of people choose to express their beliefs about life and their relationship to the source of life (Higher Power or God) and others. One textbook definition reads: "Religions are bodies of doctrine that specify a way of life centered on the maximization of the good, where the good includes both morality and right purpose" (The Progressive Living Glossary). Some examples of religious actions would be: reading the Bible, studying religious doctrine or theology, belief in God, prayer, receiving Communion, celebrating the Seder meal at

Passover, service to others, and observing special days or periods on a religious calendar, such as Christmas, Easter, Passover, Yom Kippur, or Ramadan.

Spirituality, on the other hand, is about "growth in becoming fully human." It is related to our need to feel connected to the source of life, connected to others and the world. Spirituality implies a self-transcendence, beyond my personal world and concerns. Spirituality is related to our need for hope, finding meaning and purpose in our lives. One's spirituality asks the question, "How do I relate to the source of life, and to the rest of life?" A healthy spirituality is one that imparts a growing awareness of our interconnectedness, our essential oneness with all people, with all of creation and God. Understood in this way, everyone has spirituality, a spiritual life, a need to feel connected. Some choose to express it in religious ways and practices. Many have a belief in a Higher Power or God; some do not but still feel quite connected and whole. They love and receive love. Some deny a connection with the rest of life and the world altogether, which can be problematic.

I once heard someone describe the relationship between religion and spirituality as being like the relationship between marriage and love. It was explained in the following way: One can be married but not in love, and one can be in love but not married, or (ideally) one can be married and in love. The point is that one doesn't necessarily lead to the other. In the same way, a religious act can also be spiritual (and ideally it is) but it does not have to be.

The religious does not necessarily lead to the spiritual. Consider the people who hijack airplanes and fly them into buildings. These are very religious people. However, their violent acts against innocent life show them to be disconnected from the common good, lacking any spiritual quality at all. You may remember the Rev. Jim Jones and his followers in Guyana. I can still recall seeing the television images of him preaching to his disciples. Jones, too, was a very religious person. In the end, he and more than 800 of his followers drank poison, committing suicide in a religious act that was devoid of any spiritual connection.

Of course these fanatics are extreme examples, used to make a point. But on a more day-to-day level, have you ever known someone who, though seemingly very religious, was completely miserable to be around, negative and unconcerned with the needs of others? Again, religious actions can, and ideally do, lead one to spiritual growth and to a spiritual connection with others—but this is not always the case.

It can be very helpful to take a look at our own religious practices to see what effect they are having upon us. Ask yourself the following questions: How do my religious practices or beliefs affect the way other people feel when they are around me? Do my religious practices help me to become a more hospitable, loving, kind, and accepting person? Do they help me to have a generative attitude toward others, one that affirms and nurtures other people's growth as human beings? Or does my religion provide me with a reason to feel better than others?

The goal of any healthy religious belief is to help us to rediscover our connectedness to all of creation and recognize the spark of the divine within each person. It is to help us to realize that there are invisible ties that bind us together. In fact, the more enlightened we are, the more humble we will become. We will consider ourselves better than no one. We will notice a growing sense of gratitude and appreciation for the gracious free gift of life.

Joy is a side effect of spiritual growth. Perhaps it is more correctly called a direct effect of spiritual growth. At the end of the day, God does not want religious acts from you; God first wants a loving relationship. From that relationship, joy will well up within you and fill everything you do. Your actions, including religious acts, will transcend your mind, body, and spirit, strengthening your connection with others and with God, for they will be done in love.

CONNECTING POINT

There is a difference between knowing things about God and knowing God. From time to time, conduct a religious or spiritual self-evaluation. Are your religious beliefs and practices helping you to grow and connect spiritually with others, self, and God? This is important, because if you desire lasting joy, authentic spiritual growth is its source.

PRAYER

Loving God, who sees the thoughts behind all the things I do, help me to desire that which is good and holy in your sight. Direct my heart that I may grow in relationship with you, so the joy that can only come from knowing you will live in my heart and fill all my actions. Amen.

44 Harden not your heart

▶ RABBI AKIVA FEINSTEIN

In our journey through life, there is a tendency to enjoy the adventure, relish the delicious flavors, enjoy the sweet smells, but run as fast as we can past those things in life that cause us discomfort and pain. It is as though we instinctively separate as much as possible from the tough occurrences in life, so they do not get in the way of the life we think that we should be leading. But the difficult twists and turns in life may in fact be the most important part of the journey. They are the surest way to learn more about one's true self, and at the same time to really understand what one's relationship with God is all about.

The challenge of dealing with suffering is something about which most world religions have something to say. Each religion's view ends up being an important part of its core philosophy and belief system. Most religions began at a time in history of great suffering for certain peoples, or for the leader of the religion itself. The religion would be of little worth if it did not provide some explanation of why life is often so hard. The need for understanding about the mystery of suffering has always been part of the human condition. We search into the meaning of suffering in order that we might learn how to better deal with it. But written on our hearts is the more basic question of why pain and suffering need to exist at all.

As far back as the Garden of Eden, humans have sought the answer to that basic question. Adam and Eve ate from the forbidden fruit under a tremendous risk. They were told that if they ate from it, they would no longer be able to enjoy "eternal life" as they had until that time, but would have to go through some sort of "death" in order to acquire a new knowledge, and in the process, learn about pain, human weakness, and their own mortality. The story shows how they were willing to forfeit all of the pleasure of the Garden just to have the knowledge of good and evil.

One of the major obstacles that people have in learning about suffering is the misconception that all suffering and pain are inherently bad. Just a few simple observations about pain in other parts of our life can help us to gain a different understanding.

Pain does have a very real purpose in the human body. It eaches sufferers where to focus their energies and how much effort to expend. Were it not for pain, the central nervous system might direct us to reach into a fire to pull out a potato. Pain inhibits us to prevent catastrophe. The pain is not pleasant, but it deters us from actions that would do us much greater harm. In this way it helps to turn our distracted mind to the needs of the current moment.

Pain is a gift of divine love, but it is tough love. Adversity opens our eyes and forces us to look at the mirror of truth. It is the basis of Alcoholics Anonymous that people cannot begin to heal themselves until they realize they are in a state of despair, that they can no longer rely on illusions or preposterous hopes. When we hit bottom, there is no place else to go. The pain of despair proves to be the strongest and most clarifying motivator, and until it is activated, addicts very often are unable to muster the courage to focus and find their way out. Life is filled with stories of people who have lost it all, but rather than becoming paralyzed, are invigorated by the experience and motivated to change their lives.

Good fortune rarely leads to God. Most people are grateful, but this gratitude rarely causes us to question why we received what we have. Grief, however, leads us directly to God, to knock on the door, and ask why it has to be this way. Recall the message of the Chinese ideogram, or symbol, for "crisis" mentioned earlier. Every crisis has enshrined within it the opportunity for growth, for change, along with the inherent danger that it contains.

We may never understand the "why" of pain and suffering in our lives, why things have to be this way. But we owe it to ourselves to at least try to keep our mind and our heart open during times of pain and difficulty. It is only with an open heart that we will be able to see and hear what opportunity God has hidden in the midst of our struggle. "Oh, that today you would hear God's voice: 'Harden not your hearts'" (Psalm 95:7–8).

CONNECTING POINT

It may be difficult to believe that joy can be born out of our suffering, but it is true. Suffering is not the beginning and the end. In the end it is about spiritual growth and deepening our relationship with God, the source of true, lasting joy.

PRAYER

Lord, help me to remain open when I experience pain and suffering so that I can hear the healing word you want to speak to me. I am often tempted to close myself off, clench my fists and turn away from life and therefore from you. Help me not to harden my heart but rather to open it to your presence. Amen.

45 Life moves

discovering the freedom
to move with it

▶ RABBI AKIVA FEINSTEIN
and CHARLES W. SIDOTI

*Our world and our individual lives are in the process of
evolving....It is not a question of rejecting the past but of
letting the past flow into the present and letting this process
guide us as to how to live in the future.*   – JEAN VANIER

Pope John Paul II, speaking to church leaders about the mission
of the church, once said, "We are not here to guard a museum,
but rather to tend and nurture a flourishing garden." These words,
spoken by one of the most popular and influential popes in modern
history, eloquently describe the importance of having a healthy,
positive attitude toward the constant change that is part of our lives.
Referring to the church, his words challenge those who want their
church, temple, synagogue, or mosque to remain as they have always
known it to be, believing that it should not change in any way.

Life moves. It is not the nature of life to be static. Think about
it, has your life ever stopped changing? New things, people, and

163

happenings are constantly coming in and out of our lives. We are personally affected by the continual movement and evolution taking place in the world. Sometimes these changes take place slowly, sometimes in the twinkling of an eye. Have you ever had the experience of looking at an old photo of yourself and trying to remember what you were thinking at that time? It is impossible, because you simply are not there anymore. You have changed and moved on from that place and time. And you will continue to change and to move on from where you are now. It is a good idea to come to terms with this most basic, inescapable fact about life: It moves. Whether you realize it or not, this is a very positive truth. Understanding it is crucial because much of our struggle comes from our resistance to life's continuous movement into the future.

Sometimes our response to this constant change is to cling inordinately to people or things, those we already know, those who are already part of our life, the status quo. Fearing the unknown, which is inherent in all change, we try to hold on to what is familiar as we stand before an uncertain future. Doing this, however, comes with a price. In the words of Jean Vanier:

> If we try to prevent, or ignore, the movement of life, we run the risk of falling into the inevitable depression that must accompany an impossible goal. Life evolves; change is constant. When we try to prevent the forward movement of life, we may succeed for a while but, inevitably, there is an explosion; the groundswell of life's constant movement, constant change, is too great to resist.
>
> – *BECOMING HUMAN*

In order to live peacefully in an ever-changing world, three things are essential: a healthy detachment, gratitude, and hope.

Detachment can be seen as a decrease in our need to hold on to anyone or anything. It is a way of thinking and being that gives us the freedom to flow with life. Detachment gives us the freedom to be open to new possibilities and newness of life after something in our life changes or dies, even when we don't understand how that newness will come to be.

Without gratitude, detachment is nothing more than indifference. To live with detachment does not mean that we simply forget and move on from the past as though everything old is bad. As in the opening quotation, it is a matter of allowing the past, with its enduring life values and principles—openness, love, wholeness, unity, peace, the human potential for healing and redemption, and most important, the necessity of forgiveness—to flow into the present and become integrated into what is happening today.

Likewise, we do not forget the loving people in our lives when they are separated from us by death, changes in circumstances, or when they can no longer serve our needs. Detachment does not mean that we cast aside material things without a thought when we no longer have use for them. Healthy detachment means that we look upon the people and material things of this life with gratitude. We realize that they are gifts received from a loving God, gifts that will ultimately return to God.

Finally, it is only possible to practice authentic detachment when we are in a real relationship with the Living God; and such a relationship is always grounded in hope. It is then that we are able to see and appreciate the people and the good things of this life for what they really are. When we really believe that it is God who is leading us, it becomes possible to let go of people and things when the proper time comes to move on in our life's journey. In this way, hope helps us to truly love and appreciate these people and things, without being possessed by them. As the words of Ecclesiastes teach us, "For everything there is a time." The nineteenth-century Christian thinker Søren Kierkegaard, in discussing how hope forms the basis for Judaism and Christianity, described hope as "divinely sanctioned optimism, sheer promise for this life."

CONNECTING POINT

Life will continue to move forward, taking us along with it, whether we like it or not. The point is that we need not be carried along kicking and screaming, fretting over and trying to control every change that comes our way. Through a healthy sense of detachment, with gratitude and hope in our hearts, we can choose to enter peacefully into the flow and evolution of life. Strive to accept life's constant change, trusting that God is present within that change, guiding you through whatever you may be experiencing.

PRAYER

Loving God, in order to move freely with you through life, I need to trust you. Give to me that trust that will carry me from yesterday to today, into all of the tomorrows of this life, and finally into eternity with you. Amen.

PART FOUR

The wonderful person God created you to be

We can be so hard on ourselves. We are only human. And yet, our humanness is the greatest gift we have received. Once we accept ourselves as wondrous and unique creations of God, flaws and all, it then becomes possible to grow more fully into the person that God is calling each of us to be. It is through the process of human growth and development, it is through trusting enough to experience our humanity to the full, that the mystery of who we really are, and who God really is, is slowly revealed. This is the spiritual journey. Real self-acceptance is a key that opens many doors. It makes it possible to love ourselves and others, and perhaps most importantly, it helps us to trust God enough to allow our lives to evolve and unfold. The reflections in this final section are written with the hope that you might realize that above all. You really are a child of God.

46 A change in the way we see ourselves

...can change the way "we see"

▶ CHARLES W. SIDOTI

What do you think other people see when they look at you? The way I think others see me can have a great impact on my self-esteem and therefore on how I experience and interact with the world around me. If I view a personal characteristic about myself in a negative way, it may cause me to feel inadequate. I may feel that I have to hide whatever I consider my flaw to be. I may see myself as being too fat, too thin, too tall, too short, too shy, too talkative, or as having some other defect or imperfection. I may even assume that others see the characteristic in the same negative light that I do. We should not be so quick to make that assumption. I have been pleasantly surprised on more than one occasion to discover that something that I had always considered unworthy about myself was actually seen by someone else in a completely different way. The following story is a great example:

I have a sizable space between my two front teeth that, unless I am laughing spontaneously, I often cover with my hand because I feel self-conscious. I don't know why I feel this way. No one has ever made fun of me because of it. But for some reason I have always felt self-conscious about it.

One Sunday, my family and I took our dog to church to take part in an outdoor event called the Blessing of the Animals, which is held in honor of the feast day of St. Francis of Assisi. After the pet-blessing ritual, I was chatting with some people and noticed a visiting priest standing nearby. I said hello to him. He extended his hand and greeted me, saying that his name was Fr. Gerald. The next words out of his mouth were, "I like the space between your teeth."

He pointed to his own teeth while referring to mine. I didn't quite know how to respond to his directness. He went on to say, quite sincerely, "It is very nice." I thought he was kidding, kind of gently making fun, but he wasn't. He continued, "I am from Nigeria. In my country people want this gap. They go out of their way to get their teeth to be this way. They will even chip their teeth to get it."

He explained that in his country, a space between the front teeth was considered a "disarming quality," something that made people feel comfortable with you. I had never thought of the space between my front teeth in that way, or in any way that was positive. But hearing his words instantly changed that, and the sincerity of his comment helped.

I realized that he was right. When I had previously met people with a space between their front teeth, it had often had a disarming effect. I almost always had found these people very friendly and comfortable to be around. Now I was able, for the first time, to see the space between my own front teeth as something good, even desirable.

Nothing has changed about the space between my teeth. The only thing that has changed is the way I see it. Because of the words of Fr. Gerald, what I previously saw as a defect, I now see as an advantage, something that can draw people in rather than make me feel different from them. Before this encounter, if you had asked me about the space between my teeth, everything I would have said about it would have been negative. I might have even mentioned to you that I had thought about getting it "fixed" someday.

Since meeting Fr. Gerald I enjoy smiling. The space between my two front teeth has had a paradoxical impact upon me. The difference between its having a negative and positive impact has been my relationship with it. A seemingly chance encounter with a Nigerian priest helped to change my perspective. I now believe most of our problems are like this one. They are at the very least two-sided, and may have a negative or positive impact upon us depending on how we choose to view them.

The fact of the matter is, we don't know how others see us; we just think we do. We often assume they see our flaws in the same magnified way that we do. It is helpful to realize that other people really are just that, other people. They have their own way of seeing the world and us too, and that way is often more kind, gentle, and accepting than we give them credit for.

It is not always this way. Yes, there are mean, negative people who go around focusing on others' defects, but most people are not like that. Tell yourself that just for today, you are not going to try to think for other people by assuming they think negatively of you. Instead, try to trust in the goodness that is inside most people by allowing them to draw their own conclusions about you. You will most likely be pleasantly surprised when you discover how you are really seen by others. It can change in a wonderful way how you see the world and yourself.

CONNECTING POINT

There is a difference between the way you see yourself and the way others, including God, see you. Reflecting on this simple truth can bring healing to your self-esteem. Have you ever been surprised to find out that something you have always judged yourself very harshly about, some flaw or defect, is not seen so negatively by someone else?

PRAYER

Loving God, Creator of all that I am, you tell me that I am your child. I don't always feel that way. Grant that I may know in my heart that I really am your child and receive the healing and peace that comes from truly believing it. Amen.

47 Already good

discovering the freedom to be who we really are

▶ CHARLES W. SIDOTI

I have found that learning to love and accept who we really are is one of the keys to real spiritual growth. The following reflection offers some insights that might be helpful to you in this regard.

Certain words and phrases have a power to motivate us to change the way we live if we are open to them, allowing their wisdom to unfold within our hearts. One such phrase is, "Your life isn't about you." I remember that when I first heard it, the phrase stopped me dead in my tracks and caused me to reflect. A statement such as this can lead us to an awareness of a world we never knew existed— God's world. It can open us to see and choose to live in God's world over our own little individual world. It can cause us to leave behind our former way of seeing life.

There are many other words, phrases, and even people that have a similar ability to help us to expand our current perspective. This potentially life-changing quality can also be found in art, music, and poetry. I refer to these kinds of words, statements, people, and art as being "full of Zen" or having a Zen-like quality. According to R.H. Blyth, "Zen is the essence of all religion, including Buddhism, Judaism, and Christianity, and it is moreover the essence of all art, poetry, music and deep life" (*Zen and Zen Classics*). We should not be intimidated by the word Zen. It is a very good word. I once wrote a research paper while in college titled "Tradition in Chinese Poetry," in which I attempted to describe this Zen-like quality:

> All Chinese poetry, all art, calls one to contemplation. It possesses a quality that communicates intuitively to the beholder. The Chinese tradition is to create with "awareness" and attentiveness to this quality they call Ch'an, in Japanese, Zen. – CHARLES W. SIDOTI

The words of Jesus are full of Zen, in that if we are open to them, they have the power to guide us to a new level of consciousness and growth. Real growth involves the movement from an ego-centered existence toward becoming a more psychologically and spiritually integrated person aware of our connectedness with others and with all of life. If we fail to grow in this way, we can live our lives trying to be something or someone we are not, and a false self evolves. Identification with a false self-image is actually quite normal, especially during adolescence and even into young adulthood, a time when we naturally search for our own personal identity. It only becomes a problem when we never grow beyond that early self-image and never evolve into maturity.

Many well-known films and stories are based on the theme of a character who emerges beyond the image of a false self through an adventure of some sort, thereby experiencing a measure of personal growth. I often think about a scene in one of my favorite children's films, *Toy Story*. It is the scene where Buzz Lightyear was forced to finally accept the fact that he was not a real space ranger as he had always thought himself to be. He was just another toy.

It was not easy for him, but as he finally accepted who he was and took his proper place, he was inwardly healed.

As Buzz realized that his life was not about him, but rather about himself in relationship to others, he found happiness and a peace he had never known before. It is also interesting that Buzz did not come to this awareness in isolation, but through his active participation in life (a cartoon life, of course) and with the help of his friend Woody. It was Woody who helped Buzz come to the realization that *being* a toy is much better than *imagining* oneself to be a space ranger.

In another well-known film, *The Wizard of Oz*, the Cowardly Lion, who had felt bad about himself, believing that he lacked courage, comes to the same realization when, near the end of the film, the Wizard says to him, "You, my friend, are a victim of disorganized thinking." Through their dialogue, the Wizard helps the lion to know in his heart that "who he is" is perfectly fine. This enables the lion to no longer need to pretend to be "The King of the Forest."

Words can help us open to a new level of conscious living by guiding us to achieve a greater personal integration and a new level of self-acceptance, enabling us to be who we really are. The important message in all of this is that you and I are already good, although we may not yet know it or believe it. The more we are able to accept ourselves as we are, flaws and all, realizing we are children of God, the more we will be able to live in the humble simplicity of this truth. As you grow in seeing yourself in this way, the less need you will have to live from an imagined center of the universe, and you can take your place in God's world.

CONNECTING POINT

The more we can be who we really are in life, the better off we will be. It sometimes takes a little courage, but the benefits of doing so far outweigh the risks.

PRAYER

Lord, open me to the greater meaning that you have for my life; show me what my life is about. Help me to grow beyond my small, personal world and its concerns, to discover who I am in your eyes and in your world. Free me from self-consciousness and from being pre-occupied with selfish misery. Help me to discover and to accept with gratitude the person you created me to be. Amen.

48

"Bake your own loaf of bread"

discovering your own unique path

▶ CHARLES W. SIDOTI

Thomas Merton once compared living a spiritual life to standing before a field of fresh fallen snow that you must cross: "Walk across the snow and there is your path." Being a trailblazer through the fresh fallen snow, as Merton puts it, involves walking your own unique, untrodden path. As good as Merton's advice sounds, it can be difficult to put into practice. Many of us would much rather walk familiar, well-trodden paths. Yet it is precisely the walking of a unique, untrodden path that each one of us, individually, is called to do in our lives if we truly desire to grow in our relationship with God and others. Reflecting on what walking your own unique path would mean in your life can make all the difference in the world.

In considering how to follow Merton's suggestion, it is necessary to realize that it involves a paradox. None of us walks through life completely alone. We live out our lives among other people. We have all heard the saying, "No man is an island," by the great Christian poet John Donne. Hopefully, the relationships we have with others are mutually beneficial in helping us to grow and develop. On the other hand, it is also true that we are at times quite alone. Our personal moments of loneliness remind us of this truth in no uncertain terms. Taking the first step onto our own field of freshly fallen snow involves realizing this paradox and accepting it into our life. Just realizing and accepting that these two things, loneliness and our feeling of being connected with others, are a natural part of life can be helpful. There is a natural rhythm that exists between these two feelings, and sometimes one of the feelings is dominant.

It is very helpful when we discover the relationship between our aloneness and our connectedness with others, because the two work together in our lives. The relationship was explained to me in a most interesting way on one of my visits to the Abbey of the Genesee. During a conversation with Br. Anthony, I asked his advice about something I was dealing with at the time. I remember wanting him to just tell me what to do about the situation. Have you ever wrestled with a personal issue and felt as if you wanted someone else to make a decision for you? That is how I was feeling.

His answer to me was very wise. He very kindly said, "Chuck, you know it is kind of like making a loaf of bread. You can find a recipe in a book and follow it. You can ask others about how they bake theirs and learn about other interesting ingredients and get advice about how others do it. But in the end, everyone must bake his or her own loaf of bread."

After this conversation, I realized that I would not want anyone else to bake my loaf of bread—make my decisions, live my life. It is our involvement, our interaction with life, and the decisions we make that keep life fresh and alive. Once we reach the age of reason, no one can really make a decision for us. When you think about it, would you really want them to? Our lives are unique, just as we are, and therefore our relationship with life is meant to be unique. Seek out the wisdom others have to offer, yes, but realize at the same time the precious and exciting opportunity you have in your life to bake your own loaf of bread.

CONNECTING POINT

Can you see a rhythm in your life between feelings of aloneness and feeling that you are connected to others? Sometimes it is the *aloneness* part that needs attention, so that aloneness may become solitude. You can do this by seeking out a little bit of time alone each day just to be quiet or pray. Through this time, you will discover that you are never really alone.

PRAYER

Good and gracious God, place gratitude in my heart for the gift of life. In times of difficulty, I don't always see it as a gift. Sometimes it feels like a burden, especially in times of loneliness. Help me to make decisions that will lead me to the peace you desire to give me. Place in my heart the desire to bake my own loaf of bread—with you. Amen.

49 Life is too short

learning to see your life as a precious gift

▶ CHARLES W. SIDOTI

No doubt you have heard someone use the expression, "Life is too short!" The truth is that one must be happy in order to believe that life is too short. If one is unhappy, then life can seem much too long.

When I first started working at the hospital, I was twenty-seven years old and worked in the maintenance department. One of my duties was to go into patients' rooms and change the air filters in the individual heating units. This meant I had a lot of contact with patients, and sometimes I would chat with them as I did my work. I recall one elderly man in particular. During our conversation, he asked me how old I was, and when I told him he said to me very enthusiastically, "Oh, you have a long way to go! Enjoy it!"

He went on to tell me how fortunate I was to be so young and to have such a long future still ahead of me. He told me how he had enjoyed life as a young boy, swimming in rivers and having fun, and then about the many years he enjoyed working. His words were completely authentic and his sincerity was striking. For this man, life *was* too short. He was happy, and it was obvious. I thought to myself, here was a man, sick in a hospital bed, who certainly knew

179

he was approaching the end of his life and said so himself, but he was happy.

I think the reason his words made such an impression on me is because I remember that period of my life as being a rather unhappy, lonely time. Hearing this kind old man's comment lifted me up because it gave me hope, and the hope was that it was possible to end up old—and happy. When you are young and life seems difficult, that is a very good thing to know. I decided then that I wanted to be the same way when I reached his age. There are a lot of people who are old—and happy.

Consider how you might like to approach the end of your life. Would you like to have a positive attitude and feel gratitude for your life? Would you like the younger people who know you to be encouraged by your life? In the end, most of us would like to live a life that inspires hope in others. There really is no set formula for living such a life. Allow yourself be encouraged by the older people you come in contact with who still have a twinkle in their eye. They have a wonderful message to share.

The best way I know to reach the end of life happy and filled with peace is to ask God, whatever your understanding of God might be, to help you to remain open to the lessons that life has to teach you, during both the happy and the difficult times. Second, appreciate the people you know personally who seem to be living such a life. Simply taking the time to appreciate the example of another's beautifully lived life is one of the most helpful lessons we can learn. It's kind of like gazing upon a beautiful sunset. You don't do anything but appreciate it, yet somehow it reaches down inside you, touching and encouraging you from within. The sunset, by simply letting you know that such beauty is possible at the end of the day, calms, soothes, and inspires.

CONNECTING POINT

Is there someone from your past or present whose life you find inspiring? Can you identify a specific quality or virtue that you most admire in that person? What can you learn from him or her?

PRAYER

Loving God, teach me to live in such a way that I am open to learn the lessons from life that you desire to teach me, so that when my life's journey comes to an end, I will have grown into the person you have called me to be. Amen.

50 The examined life

spiritual growth through the years

▶ CHARLES W. SIDOTI

Socrates said, "The unexamined life is not worth living." While I have always considered this statement to be wise, for a long time it left me relatively unmoved. That has changed. I now find application for this incredible statement both in my personal life and in my daily work as a hospital chaplain.

Ideally, the universal wisdom found in Socrates' statement should be appreciated throughout our life, encouraging lifelong reflection and growth, helping us to become fully integrated human beings. In my work as a chaplain, I have found that for some, "The unexamined life is not worth living" does not ring true until a serious medical condition or advanced age brings the end of life within sight. At the end of life, an existential search for meaning often occurs. This search for meaning can be experienced as "spiritual distress," and feelings of sadness, depression, fear, anxiety, or guilt are often part of that.

It is helpful to remember that while religion and spirituality can be interrelated, they are not synonymous. Spirituality is about human growth and development at every stage of life. It is about our need to feel connected to the source of life, to others, and to the world. Spiritual growth implies a self-transcendence, beyond *my* personal world and concerns, that enables me to achieve meaningful personal and social integration.

Spirituality is related to our need to find hope, meaning, and joy in life. Part of my role as a hospital chaplain is to facilitate a process that helps patients examine and eventually reframe their lives, their relationships, and their illnesses. A chaplain can help a patient discover a sense of renewed meaning within a larger integrated and self-transcendent context. Ideally, my role as a chaplain is to assist patients in doing the inner work that *they* need to do. A chaplain nurtures personal growth in what it means to be fully human and fully alive. This work may involve particular religious beliefs and practices or it may not.

If it is true that the unexamined life is not worth living, what would living an examined life mean? It means making time to stop at regular intervals from our constant activity. It means finding our own unique way (prayer, quiet time, meditation, etc.) of allowing our racing minds to slow down and rest. It means finding a regular place and time to "just simply be." If you are faithful to this time that you set aside, as little as five minutes a day, you will find that the noise in your mind will lessen and the sense of urgency to complete your "to do" list will lessen as well. You will gradually become more aware of the fact that you really are not alone. You will grow in awareness of God's presence in your life.

The truth is that living an examined life is not complicated. In fact, nothing could be simpler. It is available and accessible to all who desire to live in a more harmonious way. Living an examined life does take a little effort and discipline, and, more importantly, a sincere willingness on our part. The rest is really done for us as we simply sit quietly, and what is really important in life is slowly revealed to us by a loving, compassionate God, in God's time.

CONNECTING POINT

Do not wait until you are on your deathbed before you decide to ask yourself, and ask God to show you, what is truly important in your life. Ask God to help you focus the majority of your attention and energy on those things and to enable you to let go of useless worry.

PRAYER

Lord, help me to desire and to be open to lifelong growth and to remember that it is you who guides and directs the growth process within me. Help me to live "an examined life," in little ways each day. May I more fully realize your presence in my life and my connectedness to others that I share life with; and may I experience the inner healing that comes from knowing that you have ultimate control. Amen.

51 Cut your heroes some slack!

they are not superhuman, simply human

▶ CHARLES W. SIDOTI

One of the most important revelations about Mother Teresa was made known after her death. Personal letters written by her that were made public show that she was plagued by serious doubts about her faith. The headline read: "Letters Reveal Mother Teresa's Secret: Book of Iconic Nun's Letters Shows She Was Tormented by Doubts in Her Faith." The article stated in part, "In a rare interview in 1986, Mother Teresa told CBS News she had a calling, based on unquestioned faith....But now, it has emerged that Mother Teresa was so doubtful of her own faith that she feared being a hypocrite."

At first my heart sank over this news, but as I thought more about Mother Teresa having serious doubts about her faith in God, I found myself saying, "Thank God! Finally, something I can relate to about Mother Teresa!"

As I was growing up, I remember seeing the images of her that were frequently in the news. Stories and books about Mother Teresa's dedication to the "poorest of the poor" and how she saw the face of God in the outcast and destitute of Calcutta were very popular. Pictures of her in her familiar blue-and-white habit, looking saint-like, were also common. Many times she would be holding in her arms one of the poor children she served. Seeing these images, I recall admiring her, but I also recall feeling that I simply could not relate to the saint-like behavior or the unquestioning faith that she always displayed. The iconic figure in the news just did not resonate with my faith experience, which has always contained some measure of doubt.

One of the things common to our perception of religious figures, whether they be found in Scripture or in contemporary society, is that they can appear to have superhuman qualities. They can seem larger than life, having an inside track to God that you and I do not have. This can cause us to falsely believe that they did not (or do not) have the same human limitations that you and I must contend with.

It must be remembered that most of the religious people that we look up to are first and foremost human. If they were not, then they really would have little to offer us, for they would not have walked the path of life in the same way that we must walk it. If Mother Teresa were more than human, then I could never hope to have her level of faith, any more than I could hope to fly like Superman. But thankfully that isn't the case. She and other great religious figures were (and are) human, and that is very good news.

The revelations about Mother Teresa's doubts do not alter my belief in God nor my admiration of her virtuous, God-centered life. They confirm it. The simple truth is that faith must co-exist with doubt or it cannot be called faith. Faith without doubt, or at least the possibility for doubt, is something else—fanaticism or extremism possibly, but it is not faith. The God that Mother Teresa professed belief in is not an otherworldly pie-in-the-sky god but rather a God whose presence transcends and envelops, who comes to us from within creation yet can seem hidden and very difficult to perceive. This is the basis of our need for faith—real, doubt-containing faith.

Consider for a moment some other well-known religious figures, people whose lives are held up as being specific examples of lives lived by faith. Do you suppose that Abraham had serious doubts? How about Moses? Gandhi? Martin Luther King Jr.? If so, should we think less or more of them for having persevered in their life's work, despite their doubts? Could it not be said that the greater the personal doubt, the more virtuous the life that struggles to see the presence of God in a world that can seem so cruel, random, and chaotic, yet on the other hand can be filled with kindness, beauty, order, and wisdom? Allowing our heroes to be human— in fact, being thankful for their humanness—can be an important first step for those who hope to follow in their footsteps. Allowing them to be human helps us to allow ourselves to be human as well, and accept our own limitations. When we do this, we will more readily see the spark of the divine that exists not only in our heroes, but also within ourselves, and within all of creation.

CONNECTING POINT

The important thing is not whether you can relate to your heroes; it is hard not to see them as being superhuman. The important thing is that underneath it all, believe it or not, your heroes can relate to you. If you could talk with them, they would be the first to tell you how much like you they are—simply human. That is why they can be a source of inspiration and encouragement for us.

PRAYER

Lord, direct my heart that I may be inspired by the lives of people who are admired for their great faith. Help me to see them for who they really are, and to honor them for their total trust and surrender to you. I often doubt as they doubted. Grant that I, with your help and in your time, may persevere despite my doubts. Amen.

52 Holy places and sacred things are everywhere

▶ CHARLES W. SIDOTI

Consider for a moment the way you personally see the world. Do you see it as a good place? Can you see it not only as a place that God created, but also as a place where God dwells and is present within creation? It is a question that is worth thinking about if inner peace is something you would like to experience in this life, instead of just hoping to find it in the next. The way you see the world has a lot to do with the way you relate to your personal world, the people you share life with, yourself, and God.

A powerful and lasting insight about the connection between the way we view the world and our spiritual growth came to me while I was attending a weekend retreat several years ago. The theme of the retreat was contemplative prayer, and one of the speakers, to help make a point, made reference in his talk to holy water. If you are not familiar with holy water, it is water that has been prayed over (blessed) by a priest. It is considered a sacramental in the Catholic Church, and is also widely used in some other churches. It is used to bless, as when one makes the sign of the cross and blesses oneself upon entering or exiting church. It is also used in various church rituals. Being Catholic, I have always been familiar with and fond of the tradition of using holy water.

The point the speaker wanted to make is that when you stop and think about it, all water is holy. It is holy because God made it. Water is what God knows water to be, and therefore it is holy. Understood in this way, the question could be asked, "What water is *not* holy water?" The implications of this insight are tremendous. Realizing that all water is holy has helped me to become aware in a practical way that holiness, God's presence, is not only to be found in places or things considered holy. Understanding that all water is holy, and held in existence, by God's creative love, I realized that the same is true for all of creation. It has helped me to see all of creation as a sacred and holy place, a place where God is present. This realization provides a real reason to look for God in daily life. It changes everything.

Living life at God's speed is a lot easier when you realize that the world in which we live is the place where God dwells. A healthy spiritual outlook is one that informs us that we are here to live to the fullest, not that we should rush through life on our way to something better. Belief in an afterlife and the wonderful promise that various religions proclaim about it is indeed a great consolation. It provides a great source of hope, for it is true that our time in this world is limited. However, if such a belief is to be of any real benefit, it must never imply a discounting of this life, God's presence in it, or our responsibility to be active participants in this world. God is present to us today and invites us to experience healing and peace, and to live in hope. A healthy spiritual outlook is one that gradually helps us to understand that there is more to this life than meets the eye. Such a spiritual life helps us to realize the wisdom of Thomas Merton, who once said, "We already have what we seek. It was here all the time, and if we give it time it will make itself known to us."

Remember that the water that rains from the sky, runs through the rivers and streams near your home, washes your dishes and fills your cup, is holy water. It is holy because it is part of God's creation. In the same way, all of creation is holy; it is full of God's presence, goodness, and uncreated energy that holds everything in existence.

CONNECTING POINT

Every day is a holy day because all days are God's, and God is present within it.

PRAYER

Loving God, Creator of the Universe, help me to see my life with new eyes, that my heart may be open to receive the hope, healing, and peace that you make available to me—today. Amen.

53 Looking back —from the moon!

▶ CHARLES W. SIDOTI

One of the most enlightening films I have ever seen is Ron Howard's 2007 documentary *In the Shadow of the Moon*. In the film, Apollo astronaut Jim Lovell reflects upon his amazing experience of looking back at the Earth while orbiting the moon. Lovell explains how, as he looked out the window of the spaceship and raised his hand in front of his face, the Earth appeared so small that he was able to block it out completely behind his thumb. What a perspective! I have done that same thing with my thumb while looking up at the moon on a summer evening—but Lovell's experience is something completely different.

Imagine all of Earth's history—billions of years of evolution; plant, animal, and human life; every conflict; every joy and every sorrow ever experienced; every person who has ever lived—blocked out of existence with your thumb! But you remain! It is only within the last forty out of the billions of years of our world's existence that it is even possible for anyone to see it from such a perspective and share the experience with the rest of us.

To paraphrase Lovell, from that unique perspective he realized the insignificance of Earth and all that goes on here. At the same time, however, awareness of the awesome significance and privilege it is to live as a human being on Earth rushed in upon him. In the same moment, he realized that there is nothing insignificant about human life on Earth. Lovell was able to see the great paradox of our life in a way that only the few human beings who have been to the moon have seen it.

In the same documentary, Apollo astronaut Gene Cernan shares the fact that through the experience of going into space and looking back upon the Earth, he came to the personal realization that the universe is made with too much purpose, contains too much beauty, and is too complex to have happened by chance. In his words, "There must be a Creator that stands above the religions we have created to govern ourselves." Edgar Mitchell, of Apollo 14, reflects that the experience of leaving the Earth provided him with an epiphany, an insight into the oneness of creation. He states that through this experience, he gained an intuitive awareness that the molecules in his own body and those of the sun, the moon, and the stars, all of life on earth and far beyond, are all connected. They are one.

These awe-inspiring insights provide a beautiful context in which to reflect upon your own life. Regardless of whatever physical, mental, or emotional flaws or struggles you may have, realize that the same God who created the beauty of the universe created you. More importantly, know that you are an inseparable part of this universe. You are not separate from the rest of creation, and believing that you are is an illusion.

Be gentle with yourself. As human beings, we are all at different places and stages of our life journey and spiritual awareness. Spiritual growth is about growing in the awareness of God's presence and our essential connectedness, our oneness, with all of creation; and this takes place throughout our entire life, and in God's time.

CONNECTING POINT

Imagine orbiting the moon and looking back toward Earth. The Earth appears so small that you can hold up your hand and block it out with your thumb. The billions of years of earth's evolution, plant and animal life, civilizations that have come and gone, every person that has ever lived, every struggle, every disaster and every joy, are blocked out of existence by your thumb, and you remain.

PRAYER

Creator of the universe, my Creator, thank you for the precious gift of life. Help me to appreciate the great privilege it is to live each day. Give me the ability to reach beyond myself and to grow in awareness of your loving, supportive presence in my daily life. Instill in my heart a greater sense of gratitude for the significance of all life and indeed all of creation, of which I am inseparably a part. Amen.

54 The power of awe

▶ RABBI AKIVA FEINSTEIN

Imagine standing at the rim of the Grand Canyon, with a majestic purple-and-orange sunset blazing across the western sky. You stand transfixed. Looking up at the awesome expanse of stars, you are transformed, and lifted up in a sense of awe. Awe is an experience so powerful that it is paralyzing. At the same time, we know awe to be exhilarating, in that it makes us consciously aware of a power infinitely greater than ourselves.

Looking up at a blanket of stars, we see power, beauty, and harmony. We realize that each tiny star is actually a raging furnace. In the face of such tremendous force, we feel insignificant by comparison. We realize our own weakness, our smallness, and our mortality.

Yet the conscious realization of our smallness doesn't depress us; it inspires us! Why? Because the experience merges us with the greater whole of which we intuitively know we are a part. It assures us at our deepest level that we are not alone. The sense of awe can be a source of tremendous positive healing energy, because it makes us aware of our essential connectedness with all of creation.

There is a subtler, quiet awe to life as well, and it can come from a spring walk through the forest, a babbling brook, majestic music, a baby laughing, a heartbeat. There are so many ways that life can touch and heal us, if our hearts and minds are open to receive what these experiences have to offer.

We've all had awesome moments: witnessing the sheer power of nature in a storm, an avalanche, or fifty-foot waves on the ocean. Yet too often we leave the awesome experience and slip back into our mundane routine with the experience having little lasting impact.

Capturing the "wow"

A powerful moment of awe in my life was the birth of my first child. Leeba was born five years ago, but the electricity—the excitement, the nervousness, the sheer amazement—that I felt on every inch of my skin and deep inside has never left me. I can still recall so clearly that drive to the hospital, every turn, and every scream of my wife as labor went on. The sense of nervousness and eagerness as the moment came closer and closer. Every moment of the delivery, and, ultimately, exactly how she felt in my arms. I can recall those events as though they had just happened. I remember just how heavy she was, how she fit into my arms, her ruddy complexion, her squishy face, and, most importantly, my joy in holding the first baby in the world that was mine.

When I find myself consumed with petty anger or some selfish misery, I sometimes try to think back to that awesome moment, or another awesome moment. If I am able to connect and enter into that memory, it helps to lift me out of my narrow-minded pettinesss, if only for a second, and to move on to a more positive, less judgmental, more forgiving state of mind. An experience of awe can carry us beyond our limitations and self-centeredness by providing us with a larger perspective. When we are able to see life from such a larger perspective, our pettiness and our tendency to be judgmental toward others soften.

It is possible to live in a way in which we are more open and receptive to the awesomeness of life. It is possible to increase our exposure to it in order to enjoy its benefits more deeply. Here are a few simple suggestions that can help. First, consider how small children find everything exciting and fascinating. As adults, we tend to grow out of the childlike tendency to find amazement in life. Yet, who says that growing up must mean growing numb? Allow yourself to appreciate the miracle of it all! Decide to break the habit of always taking your daily environment for granted. Stop and consider what is taking place within and all around you.

For example, you are a human being. Stop to appreciate the fact that every aspect of our human nature is a miracle. For instance, human speech involves the coordination of lips, teeth, tongue, and larynx. Think about how the brain recalls, formulates, and transmits thoughts into muscle movements that then somehow produce sound waves that end up being our words. This is just one small part; the human body is full of amazing things, with billions of cells, each one working in harmony with all the others. I once heard someone say, "Every breath is a miracle."

The reality of the universe and our life here on earth is completely mind-boggling. We simply need to open ourselves to what is all around us to realize and experience the wonder of creation. And doing so will have an effect upon us. Making a conscious effort to do this regularly will guide you into a different way of life. It will gradually help you to live from a larger, more connected perspective. Appreciating the miracle of it all will change your way of dealing with others, your family and friends, and the way you see the environment. You will tend to be less petty and more optimistic, and find that you are more easily lifted up when you are down.

Opening yourself to the power of awe will transform you for the rest of your life.

Of course, this is not always an easy thing to do. It is certainly one of those things that are easier said than done. If we are having an especially bad day or we are in a particularly bad mood, it can be very difficult, if not impossible, to reach out of our negative state to try to focus on an awesome and positive aspect of life. We may not always be able to do so, and that is okay. That's life! Eventually, though, we will find that our bad day will give way to a new day, and our negative mood will lighten. It is important to be persistent in your effort to turn toward this tremendous source of healing energy and God's love. It will pay enormous benefits.

Finally, realize the awesomeness of you. When you see a beautiful sunset, hear a baby cry or feel the warmth of the summer sun on your face, realize that you are connected with all of this, and more, at the most intimate level of your being. You are a child of God and intrinsically a part of God's creation. Allow this truth to enter your heart and settle within you.

CONNECTING POINT

Albert Einstein once said he could never understand it all. When your attempts to figure out life and its many dilemmas fail, as they ultimately must, consider giving up the effort. Allow yourself to be amazed by life, by the wonder and awesomeness of which you are a very important and unique part. Allow yourself to be lifted up in awe.

PRAYER

Loving God, help me to realize deep in my heart at least some of what it means to be your child. Give me eyes to see you in all of creation. Help me to realize that what I see as the ordinariness of my daily life is really not ordinary at all, for you are in all things, you created all things, and life itself is a miracle. Amen.

55 Wag more, bark less

hospitality and spiritual growth

▶ RABBI AKIVA FEINSTEIN
and CHARLES W. SIDOTI

My father, Charles Sidoti Sr., was one of the most peaceful people I have ever known; he was also one of the most hospitable. On good terms with everyone, he always greeted people with a friendly smile. Everyone liked my dad. I think it was because he made them feel comfortable.

I recall times from my childhood when we would be on an elevator together or standing in line waiting our turn to get into some type of event, and Dad would often initiate a conversation with someone standing nearby. He felt comfortable enough to speak to a total stranger just to be friendly. He would make a comment about the weather or some current event. Often the conversation included a corny joke and laughter. Most people responded to him so well that I would eventually have to pull at his hand to get him away from the person he was talking to so we could get to where we were going. In his own simple way, Dad was able to achieve almost instant familiarity with strangers by breaking the silence that so often keeps us apart. It was a sincere and natural form of hospitality that I try to emulate in my own life.

Much of our time is spent in close proximity to other people. Things like going to school or work, shopping at the grocery store, or going to a place of worship, all of these bring us into close contact with others. Yet much of the time, we only really engage with those we already know or happen to work directly with. We may greet a stranger, but often that is just in passing, a fleeting acknowledgement while we continue on our way to something or someone else. To a great extent, this is completely natural and perfectly fine. We cannot expect to actively engage and interact with every stranger we walk by or happen to cross paths with. But it is worth some self-examination as to how open or closed we are to receiving strangers into our lives. There is a strong spiritual implication found in the way we relate to strangers.

The whole point of practicing a religion or of having a spiritual outlook toward life is to help us to connect spiritually with God, other people, and the world around us. Genuine hospitality is one of the keys to authentic spiritual growth, in that it helps us to connect with other people. Practicing hospitality leads to the expansion of our conscious awareness beyond our own familiar environment, reaching out to others in their world and welcoming them into ours.

People respond to hospitality. Have you ever experienced a day when you felt so good inside it showed on your face? Maybe something really good happened to you, or something you had been looking forward to was about to happen. For whatever reason, on that day you had a smile on your face, a distinctive glow about you, and you cheerfully greeted others. On such a day, the world seems to be a friendlier place. It isn't your imagination; there is a reason why you experience the world differently when you feel good.

Recall the old adage "Laugh and the world laughs with you, cry and you cry alone." Often dismissed as trivial or trite, most clichés actually contain a kernel of truth that can direct us to an important life principle. This one certainly does. When you feel good, you give off positive vibrations that people perceive, and they are therefore naturally drawn to you. When you are angry or otherwise feeling bad, you give off negative vibrations, and people are naturally repelled. Think about it: Do you enjoy being around someone who smiles, is friendly, open, and welcoming? Or do you like to be around someone who is often very intense, complaining, and frowning much of the time?

Important spiritual insights can come from all parts of life, even from the animal world. On my way to work one morning, I observed a bumper sticker that creatively focused on the importance of communicating positively with others. It said, "Wag more, bark less." I very quickly thought of a dog, as you most likely did. This simple statement contains a great truth that can be very helpful to us if taken to heart. Dogs have a way of winning people over. (Not all people, of course; there are some people who simply don't like dogs, and it's okay if you are one of those people.) By and large, people like dogs. The reason is dogs' unconditional love, the friendly affection they naturally give and so freely convey to humans. Dogs relate so well to people that they are used for therapy in hospitals and nursing homes. Petting a dog, or simply being around one, has been shown to lower blood pressure and lifts the human spirit.

When a dog wags its tail in our presence, it is communicating with us in a visible and powerful way. It is conveying its inward happiness in a way that we instantly understand. Most often we respond by petting the dog or speaking kindly to it. The opposite happens when a dog barks or growls at us. It is conveying its displeasure, again in a way that we instantly understand. We react by moving away or by protecting ourselves in some way. As humans, we do the very same thing, just differently. We, like dogs, express our inner feelings in a visible way that others instantly under-stand. We do it through our facial expressions, body language, and speech; and they have the same powerful effect as the dog wagging its tail or barking.

In large part, dogs' hospitable nature is built in; they are hard-wired, pre-programmed, to be friendly. Compared to people, dogs are simple, uncomplicated creatures. But that does not mean we cannot learn a valuable lesson from them. For some humans, like my father, hospitality also seems to come naturally. The rest of us have to work at it. Learning to practice hospitality can be challenging.

One reason it may be difficult for us to reach out to others is that in our human brokenness, caused by past hurts or rejections, we may have come to believe that we have nothing to offer. We may believe that our attempts to reach out to others will be rejected. The truth is otherwise. This world is full of people who would love and welcome your expression of hospitality. It may take courage, and yes, there is always the risk of rejection. Not everyone responded favorably to my father's hospitable nature, but most people did. There is certainly a risk involved in reaching out, but the benefits you stand to reap make it a risk worth taking.

God is hospitable. If it is true that hospitality is vital to human interactions and relationships, it follows that it would be an impor-tant part of how God chooses to relate to us. It is clear in many places in the Bible that God acts with incredible hospitality toward human beings. For instance, the book of Genesis (17:1–24) tells the story of Abraham, who at age ninety-nine undergoes circum-cision, and needless to say, has a very difficult healing period. Though he likely received many human visitors to help comfort him in his pain, the Bible tells us that was visited by none other than God. In the story, God does not simply bestow a blessing, or even send a miraculous cure, but instead graces Abraham with a personal visit.

More than a moving story, this becomes the basis for the biblical commandment to visit the sick. Sacred Scripture is filled with examples of God's hospitality toward humankind and all of creation. In Judaism, Rav Dimi of Nehardea, in the Talmud, said: *Hachnasat orchim*, Hebrew for the welcoming of guests, "is more important than study, or even the worship of God." The Russian writer Leo Tolstoy once commented on the command to welcome the stranger: "'Love the stranger and the sojourner, Moses commands, because you have been strangers in the land of Egypt.'" In Christianity, Jesus used the parable of the good Samaritan as an example of God-like hospitality for us to follow. We can draw enormous personal benefit by finding ways to imitate God's hospitality, found so often in sacred Scripture, in our daily interactions with others.

God's hospitality is not only found in the pages of the Bible, but is readily visible in the way the world was created. Sure, life is difficult and full of challenges, but it is also filled with things that did not have to be made so good, so tasty, so enjoyable, for any other conceivable purpose than to show God's divine hospitality to the world's inhabitants.

So much in this world seems to have been tailor-made for human enjoyment. The way something is created (designed) often expresses the hospitality of the creator. Consider something as simple as a banana. The potassium, other nutrients, and the relatively few calories found in this fruit could easily be provided in a tiny, tasteless berry that you could pop into your mouth. But instead, God wanted to put a lot more into the package. It is made not only to be healthy; a banana has a lovely sweet taste that does not have to be there. Next, any eater of a banana would need to know when it is ripe, so included in its packaging is a "high-tech" color sensor that tells you, to the day, when it is ready to be eaten. If you don't have a plastic bag to protect your food when you toss it into your knapsack on the way to work, a banana has a built-in carrying case. It can be eaten by anyone from a baby to an adult human or a hungry monkey, due to its ease in being mashed up or cut into bite-size pieces.

There is a beautiful Christian song, written by Dawn Thomas, called "That's How Much I Love You." It's like a love song by God to us, about how all the beautiful things in creation were made out of God's love for us. Max Ehrmann's great poem "Desiderata" explores the individual's place in creation, but it concludes with advice about the need for happiness. Do the best you can to put this advice into practice by reaching out in hospitality to others, in your own unique way, even though you may be hurting inside. This won't solve all your problems, but it will not add to them in the way having a bad temperament or openly displaying a bad mood often does. When we "wag more and bark less," feelings of isolation and separateness slowly begin to lose their grip. People respond to us differently because we are more pleasant to be around.

CONNECTING POINT

Nurturing a spirit of hospitality within yourself can be very helpful in discovering the wonderful person God created you to be. Hospitality is very much an attribute of God. Growing to be more God-like, acting in union (more often) with God's creative love and welcoming spirit, can only lead us closer to God, to others, and to all of God's creation.

PRAYER

Gracious God, Creator of all that is, help me to hear and respond to your welcoming call, your gentle embrace in my life, and to respond with that same love toward others. Give me the courage to reach out to other people, in their world, and to sincerely welcome them into mine. Help me to realize that everyone I meet is truly my brother or sister and that you are God of us all. Amen.

56

Reflect upon three things

▶ RABBI AKIVA FEINSTEIN
and CHARLES W. SIDOTI

The story is told of a Russian man walking along a city street in the Communist era who witnessed the following scene: A worker with a shovel dug a hole in a stretch of dirt bordering the boulevard, after which a second man with a shovel filled in the very same hole with the very same dirt. The onlooker ran up to the two workers and exclaimed, "Comrades, this is madness! What in the world are you doing?"

The first worker calmly explained. "Usually I dig a hole, Ivan plants a tree in the hole, and Misha fills in the dirt around the tree. But today Ivan is out sick. So what are we supposed to do? Merely because Ivan isn't here today, should Misha and I just sit around?"

How often do we find ourselves so caught up in the activity of the moment that we forget the reason for what we are doing? In our automatic completion of tasks, with our tight focus on the short-term work at hand, we forget what our goal really is. When this happens, it is very easy to miss the mark of being the people God calls us to be.

Few people make a conscious and determined decision to abandon good for wickedness. We don't just wake up one morning and decide that we are going to be a grumpy husband, a workaholic, or an impatient wife or mother. Rather, it is through stress, carelessness, and the need for real spiritual growth and insight, that we choose the easy or expedient path, only to recognize later, and often too late, the error of our ways. It is in losing touch with the big picture, what is really important in life, that we fall short in our behavior. In many ways, this is simply part of being human. It is something we need to accept and even love in ourselves, while at the same time realizing our need for growth and transformation, by which we will become more fully developed and spiritually connected with others and the world around us.

What causes our shortsighted, task-oriented behavior? It is because we often find ourselves in the midst of our journey through life without any real sense of who we are, from where we have come, or where we are ultimately going. In a real way, we need to know why we are traveling. What is the point of our journey? Why did we set out in the first place? Without an answer to these questions, even if that answer is simply a vision or an ideal, we have no motivation to carry on to the very end.

The wisdom and advice of Akavya ben Mehalalel, a leading first-century Talmudic Palestinian scholar, can be very helpful in this regard. The Mishna (a major work of rabbinic Judaism of that era) draws on his teachings, saying, "Reflect upon three things: From where have you come, from a putrid drop; to where are you heading, to a place of dust, worms and maggots; and before whom will you give an accounting..." (Ethics of the Fathers, 3:1).

From where have you come, from a putrid drop

Popular science fiction writer Robert Heinlein told of a sad little reptile that bragged he was a brontosaurus "on his mother's side." Many people, like the little lizard, have a natural predisposition toward feeling that they are not good enough the way they are. We may look for some talent or quality in ourselves by which we can inflate our own importance, instead of simply accepting who we really are. Humanity as a whole expresses this when we imagine ourselves as the crowning glory of all the generations that preceded us, occupying our rightful place at the pinnacle of creation. Someone once said that each generation sees itself as "the generation that has finally arrived."

It can be very spiritually healthy, as well as mentally healthy, to consider often from where you have come. Every one of us can trace his or her origins back to a few milliliters of seminal fluid and to a single spermatozoon. And what if another in the fertilization of our mother's ovum had edged out that particular spermatozoon? Quite simply, we would not exist, and another would occupy our place in the world. It is a very humble beginning indeed, but it is not a cause to feel inferior. In fact, the opposite is true.

It is for very good reason that the Mishna says, "Contemplate your own insignificance, if not for the divine hand that brought you into being." The important point in all this is that the divine hand *did* bring you into being. The miracle of life occurred, and continues to take place within you as your life evolves. There is no need to convince yourself (or others) that you are "a brontosaurus on your mother's side." You already are the wonderful person God created you to be.

To where are you heading, to a place of dust, worms, and maggots

As the title suggests, the 1977 song "Dust in the Wind," written by Kerry Livgren and made popular by the rock group Kansas, is a musical meditation on the impermanence of life. This once very popular song, through its haunting lyrics, conveys to us the same great truth that Akavya ben Mehalalel suggests we think about.

Our physical bodies shall indeed return to the earth from which they came, but what is the point in our thinking about it? Why would the Mishna suggest our reflecting upon it? It is not for any morbid purpose or to depress us. Rather, remembering this truth is beneficial because of the perspective for living that it can provide. The awareness of our ultimate return to dust can cause enough discomfort within us (sometimes called existential suffering) to cause us to search for a meaning beyond ourselves. We reach out for something beyond the temporal meaning that we project onto life, something beyond our projects, our desires, even beyond our good intentions. Remembering that you are dust can help you to get in touch with your "creaturehood," thereby giving you reason to reach out to the "creator."

And before whom will you give justification and accounting…

When we sincerely reach out for the creator we discover that there really is a God. We realize that God is not a fairy tale for children or the product of humanity's collective psyche, something that we created to make us feel better in a huge evolving universe. In reaching out beyond ourselves we become aware of the Living God who fills the universe and our very selves.

When this happens we are faced with a decision both awful and wonderful at the same time. The choice becomes "Whom shall we serve?" What will our lives be mostly about? Will my life be about growing in relationship with God, learning how to love and living in harmony with others? Or will it be about getting what I want while looking out for Number One? Recall the message of Reflection Twenty-Five, *You Gotta Serve Somebody*, which focused on the following statement from Scripture, "If it does not please you to serve the Lord, decide today whom you will serve" (Joshua 24:15).

Indeed, life does have real meaning and purpose, but only if we are able to know intuitively that there is more to life (and death) than meets the eye. Spiritual growth is about nurturing and developing our inner resources, by which we transcend the limitation of our senses, recognizing that there is another plan besides ours, God's plan. It is God's plan that placed us here in this temporal existence, and for a reason. God knows that reason or purpose already, but it comes to us only gradually, day by day and even moment by moment, in the living out of our lives. The ultimate meaning of our lives is beyond the ability of our minds to comprehend. That being said, there are things we do know about God's plan for us.

We know from the teachings of the major religions that God desires that we learn to live peacefully with each other, and moreover that we learn to treat others the way we ourselves want to be treated. It is certainly part of God's plan that we learn to love others, God, and ourselves. Much of what happens in life ultimately has to do with our learning what it really means to love. The difficult part is that this involves giving up our own selfish desires, which often cause us to fall short or miss the mark of being the people God calls us to be.

But missing the mark sometimes is also part of the process, and it is okay. It simply means that we are human. God accepts us as we are and continues to call us day by day. It is in continually responding to God's call that we will gradually discover the living presence of God in creation, and the important place we have been uniquely chosen to occupy in God's world.

CONNECTING POINT

Reflecting upon our own insignificance is valuable, inasmuch as it causes us to "reach out" to meet and acknowledge the Living God in our lives. One indicator of spiritual growth is increasingly seeing God's presence reflected in the created world, including within ourselves, who have been made in God's image.

PRAYER

Dear Lord, though I may not comprehend the full meaning and purpose of my life at this time, you do. Let that be enough for me. Increase in me the desire to grow in relationship with you and to learn what it really means to love as you love. Amen.

Conclusion

▶ CHUCK SIDOTI

I once heard a story about a mother camel and her baby. The baby camel asks, "Mom, why do we have these huge, three-toed feet?" The mother replies, "To enable us to trek across the soft sand of the desert without sinking."

"And why do we have these long, heavy eyelashes?" the baby camel continues.

"To keep the sand that blows with the wind out of our eyes on the trips through the desert," replies the mother camel.

"And, Mom, why do we have these big humps on our backs?"

The mother, now a little impatient with the baby, replies, "They are there to help us store fat for our long treks across the desert, so we can go without water for long periods."

"OK, I get it, Mom!" says the baby camel. "We have huge feet to stop us from sinking, long eyelashes to keep the sand from our eyes, and humps to store water. Then why the heck are we here in the Toronto Zoo?"

As human beings living in today's complex, fast-paced modern world we are much like that baby camel in the zoo. The moral of this story is that the desert experiences of our own lives, though difficult, are necessary and important for our growth. The sometimes harsh, lonely times that we all experience have much to teach us about who we really are, and who God really is. We, like the baby camel, need the desert.

Your own personal desert experience might be the desert of sudden personal tragedy, loneliness, illness, unemployment, relationship issues, addiction, depression, anxiety, or anything else that causes you to feel spiritually distressed, confused, and lost. A primary goal of this book is to help you to realize that it is often in the desert experiences of our lives that we are able to hear God's voice most clearly. The reflections are intended to help you to approach your own desert experiences with less of a sense of panic or worry and more of a sense of awe, wonder, and trust. I hope that reading this book will help you to give God your full attention as you search for meaning and hope during the times in life that you have no choice but to wait. Finally, I hope that you will hear the wonderful message God has to tell you about who you really are in God's world. Although our personal desert experiences often seem quite barren, if we can learn to listen and be attentive for signs of God's presence we may find these desert experiences to be some of the most fertile ground of our life's journey.

Kris Kristofferson wrote and published an amazing song, "The Pilgrim," in 1971. Using incredibly insightful lyrics, Kristofferson describes the character the song is about as possessing within him a multitude of contradictions. Parts of the character's personality, or being, are true, and other parts are false. Yet somehow, it is through these conflicting parts co-existing within him that he is ultimately led in the way he should go. Thinking about my own spiritual journey, and the person I know myself to be, I can relate to this character's inner contradiction. Perhaps you can, too. The words of this gritty song are quite prophetic, expressing, at least in part, what it means to be human.

When I read the words of my own reflections, I sometimes say to myself, "Who is this person who writes about how to experience inner peace, waiting in hope, responding with trust, and living in harmony with others? Is this the Chuck I know?" When I look at my own inner life, I realize that I spend much of my time living the exact opposite of what I write about. The important thing is that I am learning to accept even that.

If you think about it, you will discover that your own life involves the same stark difference between the person you know yourself to be, the person you want to be, and the person you are still becoming. A helpful way to look at the lessons and insights found in this book, or in any spiritual lesson, is to see them as containing ideals to strive for, good things to keep in mind that can help you to regain a healthy perspective in a busy, anxious, and often lonely world.

Above all, it is important to remember to be gentle with yourself. The spiritual journey is ultimately about the transformation of our minds and hearts, and a new awareness of God's presence in our lives. For the most part that is God's business, and surely God will deliver. We simply need to let it happen at God's speed and in God's time.

Notes

R.H. Blyth, *Zen and Zen Classics* (New York: Random House Inc., 1978), p. 9.

Kathleen Brehony, PhD, from a presentation given at Metro Health Medical Center, Cleveland, OH: May 2004.

Saskia Davis, *The Symptoms of Inner Peace*, 1984.

Anthony de Mello, *One Minute Wisdom* (New York: Doubleday, 1986), p. 11.

Edward F. Edinger, *Ego and Archetype: Individuation and the Religious Function of the Psyche* (New York: Penguin Books, 1972), Part 1, "Individuation and the Stages of Development."

Erich Fromm, *The Heart of Man* (Harper Colophon Books, 1968), chapter 3.

Martin Buber, trans. Walter Kaufmann, *I and Thou* (New York, 1970), pp. 9-15.

Gerald May, MD, *Simply Sane* (New York: Crossroad Publishing Company, 1993), pp. 70, 73.

Thomas Merton, *The Mystic Life* (Notre Dame, IN: Ave Maria Press, audio-tape, 1985).

Henri J.M. Nouwen, *A Spirituality of Waiting* (Notre Dame, IN: Ave Maria Press, audiotape, 1985).

Joyce Rupp, OSM, *Little Pieces of Light…Darkness and Personal Growth* (Mahwah, NJ: Paulist Press, 1994).

Pierre Teilhard de Chardin, "Patient Trust" in *Hearts on Fire: Praying with Jesuits*, Michael Harter, ed. (St. Louis, MO: Institute of Jesuit Sources, 2005), p. 102.

Jean Vanier, *Becoming Human* (New York: Paulist Press, 1998), p. 13.

Robert J. Wicks, *Everyday Simplicity* (Notre Dame, IN: Sorin Books, 2000), p. 121.

Robert J. Wicks, *Spiritual Freedom* (Kansas City, MO: National Catholic Reporter Publishing Co, audiotape, 1995).

About the authors

Author **Charles W. Sidoti** is well known as a leader in the Cleveland medical and spiritual communities. Sidoti is a clinically trained, board-certified Chaplain and Coordinator of Pastoral Care at South Pointe Hospital, part of the Cleveland Clinic Health System. Sidoti completed his training in Clinical Pastoral Education (CPE) through the Cleveland Clinic Foundation, and his theological studies at Borromeo Seminary in the Diocese of Cleveland. He was granted Board Certification by the National Association of Catholic Chaplains in 2000. As a spiritual writer, he brings:

- *Clinical experience:* Fifteen years' bedside ministry: As a full-time chaplain, Sidoti offers spiritual counseling, advises people on difficult ethical decisions, offers community education, works with Alcoholic Anonymous groups, and helps to work within different hospital committees, including the Bioethics Committee. Since starting in 1996, Sidoti has developed and implemented an exemplary interfaith Hospital Ministry, consisting of forty-three trained lay people and professional clergy at South Pointe Hospital.

- *A rich contemplative spirituality:* influenced by thirty years of association with the Abbey of the Genesee, a Trappist Monastery located in New York's Genesee Valley. The Trappists are an international Catholic contemplative order of monks also known as Cistercians.

- *National speaking experience:* In 2005 he was a presenter at Streams in the Desert, the national conference of the Association of Professional Chaplains held in Albuquerque, New Mexico.

Contributing author **Rabbi Akiva Feinstein** works as a full-time chaplain at NCJW/Montefiore Hospice, a Jewish Hospice program based in Beachwood, Ohio. In this role, he offers spiritual counseling, advises people on difficult ethical decisions, offers community education, and helps to work within different sub-communities, including Holocaust survivors and Orthodox Jews. In addition, he is a member of the Jewish Federation of Cleveland's Chaplaincy group and goes to South Pointe Hospital, Cleveland Clinic Health System, and University Hospitals to visit Jewish patients on a weekly basis.